# The Wa

Guy Wilgress Hudson

**chipmunkapublishing**
the mental health publisher

All rights reserved, no part of this publication may be reproduced by any means, electronic, mechanical photocopying, documentary, film or in any other format without prior written permission of the publisher.

>Published by
>Chipmunkapublishing
>United Kingdom

**http://www.chipmunkapublishing.com**

Copyright © Guy Wilgress Hudson 2014

ISBN    978-1-78382-038-2


Chipmunkapublishing gratefully acknowledge the support of Arts Council England.

## Lost at Sea

Ok. Begin again. That's what I must do. Have done in fact. It's all about taking your time and gently winding down into the groove of the piece. Here we commence the tale. We are lost at sea. Please don't mistrust me at this early stage. Trust me like a friend and should I break that bond of trust we share and you don't trust my story then cease to call it a story at all. Call it something other than a story.

You could name it a Factory. Now there is a story. This is bad. I must admit to being a fraud. In the Buddhist sense of the word. It all looks like Lunatic ramblings already. I did believe you can't write madness. Madness writes forever. I feel the urge for a creative masturbation. So you cannot write madness; madness cannot write.

I am mad. Well my sick note that I personally carried from my good Doctors to the DSS building every month carried a diagnosis of Psychosis. So this is the beginning of my story. It's a madhouse story written by a mad man. I must remember now you can't write madness. I will try in that case to not write a mad story. I won't tell you my life story so don't worry about that one. I am mad. Ask anyone who knows me.

Actually most people that know me tend to think I'm a bit too sensible and quiet to be mad. I am really very mad. Completely insane in fact. An arch lunatic on the quiet. Please don't broadcast this and consider now that for the sake of my reputation I would rather you keep my Schizophrenic diagnosis to yourself. Just tell people I'm a bit eccentric.

I've found love. It's simply the best feeling I've had all night. That's not what this story is about though. This is the tale of a man. Understand my friends that despite your intelligence this is not my book. It's not about me. It's the story of a man like I said. His name is George. I like George. He's very malleable. He also is a bit stuck in his ways. So allow me to turn you all on with the story of George.

George lives very much in a muddle in his mind. His mind resembles a car scrap yard like those you used to see. Scrapped cars litter a yard. These are the relics of the man's past. He was a man well accustomed to popping his life into the driving seat of an old rusty rust bucket and taking her for an imaginary spin. He's really quite a man is our George. He would like to be a daredevil. George imagines many things and remembers most of what he imagines. It's just the ticket for the old fool to take a bike ride out of the village and create, create and redo a singular phantasmagorical narrative. It goes a bit like this.

George is on a strop and cycling like the clappers along a slightly descending country lane. He hears the vehicle approach from the brow of the incline. He knows the sound of the motor. It's one of those camper vans. A blue camper approaches from behind. The regular pulse of the air cooled motor reverberates in the quiet lane surrounded by fields of cereal crops. The van, as George already knows will slow down as it draws level to him. He's freewheeling now. The girl who's leaning out of the passenger window shot at our George. She shot an arrow straight through his heart. We need you George she's saying followed by you are George Lamb aren't you George?

He brings the cycle to a stop and looks at the girl. What is it you want from me? He says. To come with us now George, we need you to help us save the planet. George being George looks way out across the Cereal fields for a moment or two. I will is all he can utter. George quietly watches as the VW Camper takes off in to the azure glare in springtime. He stands with his peddle Iron between his legs and watches while the bus of fools with him on board takes off.

George is a Watchman. I am unable to fill you in about what a Watchman actually is at the moment. I confess I do not know myself. I am waiting patiently for George and the bus of fools to reveal themselves to me more explicitly. George is a mystery.

.Ulysses, it must have taken ages to write at the pace Joyce claims to have taken in editing. The attention to detail is cited as whatever, I don't want to get distracted by even attempting to do any research about this one. I am still so determined to write something worth publishing off the top of my head it would become an obsession.

What can I say? I'm fed up with it. Smoking, drinking, woman, stopping up all night before fighting a path through the day. Things seem less offensive in the daylight hours although the cut feels much deeper if you must stand there and look at it.

Already I think I must find a workable pattern. I have always longed to write and right now I am. I want to be honest with you about this work of fiction. I find it challenging to write. Before gaining a fairly poor Upper second class BA (Hons) in English I have failed GCSE English Literature at least four times; English Language about three if you were to include the dropping out or being thrown out of colleges. That does not mean that I am an egomaniac as one time I did try really hard to pass the GCSE English yet failed. It was during a year spent living with a Cat and dying with a Dog I completed the Access to H.E course. The course runs alongside A level targets to Pass. I passed the course having achieved a Pass at English and History yet during my time on the course I studied towards GCSE English at the same time and I still failed to pass.

Now I need to tell you all so that you fully understand that I am Schizophrenic of the Paranoid persuasion. It's not my problem. If you happen to represent society then by some degree of definition you must now look away for what I am about to tell you would make you unhinged yourself. Believe me when I suggest that psychosis is like sinking in an ocean of dreams. Actually what I meant to suggest is this - It's your problem. So what if I am Schizo, mental, oh look here comes Mencap. Mencap don't even deal with the Mentally Ill that's Mentally Handicapped. Whatever you feel like calling me isn't an issue with me. Your labels put me in my place. The term Manic Depressive changed its name years ago to better describe itself. Now we all say Bi-Polar and everybody has a vague awareness of what the nutters are on about. Now forgive me if I am wrong, however the title Paranoid Schizophrenia is of course completely self-explanatory. We all know the meaning of that word. A phrenetic mentalist. Why does society or whoever it is that changes names make an effort to sort that one out. I speak it under my breath, with my hand over my mouth. Best not talk about it hey. You can call me whatever you want to be fair.

My calling okay? To write a great work of fiction. This here what you read now is yet another attempt to achieve this goal. I did write before being diagnosed. I find it difficult to construct a letter to my friend despite attempting to. I simply cannot write anything much that's comprehensible. However, all I have ever really desired is to do this. I don't know if it will happen before or after my passing. It does not matter. I may not achieve it at all. That does not matter now. I have wasted years of my life with drugs, hospital wards and porn on the internet.

I must do this. I feel like a man trying to walk with no legs. It's a story about you guys.

There is someone out there living my life. My life is being lived by a rising star of the poetry elite. It's not a place I could even get a visitors pass. It's not important from which angle you may look at me I am a Loony. But, and I mean but, he is living my life. The one I imagine myself would have lived had it not been for Paranoid Schizophrenia. Does anybody know what that actually means?

I can assure you all right now that you need not panic. No one out to get me I mean it's not like I'm vulnerable or too trusting.

## The Watchman

I want to be on the other side of the world right now. To not know anybody or be recognised in the street. That wonderful sense of lost invigorated by excitement. That's just a con, or so we are led to believe. Do you know people from elsewhere who have travelled here to England? Do they look as though they have a good time?

I want to keep this clean, clinical and free from desire.

The truth is out there. That was the voice of intuition. I tend to think not. My eyes look in and out. It's a symptom of psycho vision. It's like a see saw raising and decreasing its great trajectory. There is a lack of depth perception for the Schizophrenic.

Schizophrenia is primarily a sensory misunderstanding. Yet so frequently a Psychiatrist will look at the brain and prescribe sensory inhibitors that channel communication messages back and forth. It's our senses that are the problem not the brain. Schizophrenic misreads language. Like the lack of depth perception visually a sufferer with hearing voice disorder struggles to comprehend the audial stimulus. It's like sound through diffusion.

I have run away from that. All that anger and abuse. I have uttered these words many times and now I can say it once more. The good doctor gives me tablets to keep me quiet. I take them to keep him quiet. Why should I. Are you with me on this one? We're all crazy right. Now let's decide should we all be on this medication that can stabilise our mood and temperament to a condition of being in an emotional doldrums baking on the equator.

I have been asking my good doctor to support me with a medication holiday for years and have been declined. I am aware that every few years it is advisory to have a break from anti-psychotic medication. It has been those years and those again since I have been medication free now.

I have many obstacles before me. I cannot spell; I don't know how to structure a sentence together. My poor concentration means I won't edit much and even though I have a mind of a perfectionist I am inherently lazy. My main disability being my obsession with porn on the internet, I turn on my lap top with the intention of writing and just get completely side tracked by the internet. It's so frustrating now; I could do without the flaming internet to be honest. At least when I want to get on with my great work of fiction.

The plot of the story is simple. They always are.

I haven't been writing for a few days now and have forgotten what this particular great work of fiction is supposed to be about. I can't honestly remember. If I can keep up this sustained piece of literature for at least sixty thousand words then maybe some Mental Health Publisher will look kindly on me and publish it. A bit like getting sympathy sex from girls who know I take willy drooping medications.

The characters are dolts. It's mainly about this one middle aged man who works nights. I'm not quite sure at the moment where he works. I will get back to you on that one although it's in the middle of nowhere and a long way from where he lives.

Even now I am writing this I still have an internet page open. I keep flicking back and forth. With so little time left in my life and so much of my spare time having been so hideously wasted trawling through porn and sex profiles I am making this one last bid to achieve. This is it. My last attempt. When this one fails that's about it from me. I will retire and give in and commit myself to being an internet porn slave. I could go on to say a lot more about this. Maybe later.

This that follows is a former attempt at a great work. I changed George's name to Harold to keep him anonymous.

The Watchman

Guy Wilgress Hudson

## Burning the Midnight Oil

Harold found it hard to do his work on this occasion. He actually found it tough to do his work on most nights recently. He was thinking. Harold was doing a lot of thinking at the moment. Recently he was thinking about a lot of stuff. Most of what he thought is detritus. That's what I think. I know what he's thinking and can assure you that most of what Harold thinks is bloody rubbish. I know. It's me who has to sit and listen to the hum drum of his mind all night. You see, he thinks very loudly and I, I write Poems. This is my most recent poem. I will show it to you if you would like to read it. I'm a bit shy about the Poetry thing; it does not suit my occupation. Here it is anyway.

**The First Kiss Goodbye**

We drank wine
We kissed
Our first and last
So it seems
A long time waiting
Its coming was divine
It was unbeknown to me
Your goodbye.
My arm, my arm
Slunk with ease around your thigh
A hand, my hand
Could feel between you.
It was love like I told you
Like I never felt before
It was so long to fruition
I forgot it always was.
A kiss, our kiss; my lips touching yours
Waited for and longed for before
You said no more.
I love you I told you
So bold at last alas too late
If only I'd won a great award
If only I too was great.
I am second rate
In more ways than one.

That's about it. Rubbish really. That's what Harold and I have in common. We both keep ourselves occupied at work by doing rubbish thing's. Harold has his thoughts and I write stuff like this. It's not even a poem. I just call them poems. It impresses Harold to think he's rubbing shoulders with a real live Poet. He's never seen my poems. He thinks as I write a transcript of his inner most thoughts. Don't ask to know his thoughts. I know his thoughts and suspect he knows my poems.

Harold is deep in thought tonight; especially deep in thought. That don't mean he's having deep thoughts. Harold had a deep thought once. I would have said it was even profound, but I'd have been wasting my breath. Profound would have been a stupid word to use on a bloke like him. He'd have gone away thinking and thinking all night about it and in the morning get out a dictionary and look up profound. He would not be able to grasp the meaning. I know this as I wouldn't get it either. I ask myself is it possible to recognise something as profound without being a profound person. Profound is rubbish that's been neatly arranged into something it isn't. Harold and I, we're not profound people. Profound people do profound things.

Harold is out now doing the rounds. He likes to do at least one round a night on his own. It gives him the opportunity to think. I can see his torch light from where I am sat. He plods. He plods when we go out together and even more so when he goes it alone. He thinks he's being thorough. That's what he always says. He clomps in and shakes his muddy boots off and informs me he has been thorough. Apparently the job demands it. The job demands it.

I am embarrassed to admit to you what I do for a living. My assumption is that you have already guessed I don't make a living as a Poet. I do however spend more of my time at work versifying than I do being thorough with Harold. I'm not what I would describe as a thorough poet. More of a scribble and forget it really. A two minute wonder. For that matter two minutes could well be an exaggeration. The first time I showed my poems to someone. A girl. Her immediate response was to laugh. Great I thought she gets the joke. She said there was not a lot of meaning to it and it could do with some padding out.

**Love is you**

You gave me you so I could be young
Sucking your breast, you gave me two.
You gave me new hope as I opened the box,
You let me get naked, you gave me you.
You took me in hand I was small until
You gave me head and I gave it to you.

That was it. Not a very profound piece is it. I think not. The most profound thing is this: I don't know, that's about the best someone like Harold and I could ever know is just that. I don't know. I have read a few popular science books okay. Profound statements do not have to be true or even thought provoking. If you ever meet anyone who claims to know the truth about anything they are profane. Profane is another word my boy Harold would have to check up in the dictionary.

So would I for that matter. As a poet I would like to put forward the opinion that even the meaning of words is rubbish. To attach meaning to a word is profanity. I have heard about semiotics and multiple significations. Words mean whatever we want them to mean. That's profane, because I know I don't know. If my hunch is right then I do not know.

Thinking about it, Harold should in my opinion give up thinking. I did and it worked wonders for me. All you have to do is acknowledge the fact you know nothing. That is a fact. While I tell you about it as a matter of fact that last line could be wrong. I don't know now. I do. That's the truth; the bloody awfulness of it. I don't know I do. The facts and the truth and the impossible disintegration of all that is known and unknown.

I talk rubbish. I know this and hate it so much that it occupies my mind constantly.

The things on Harold's mind are rubbish also. His brain is more of a Massy Ferguson Tractor than a Smart Car. He's here now chugging along his country lane bouncing rhythmically up and down in the iron seat. Big heavy wheel slowly drive the vehicle past the trees and grazing animals. In our little cabin I can hear Harold's Tractor mind chugging about and I know he's bothered about something.

I could and should ask him what the matter is. You know I won't I don't need to. I'm what the matter is inadvertently. My life is our life is this life. It's all going to shit for me and he knows that and I suspect that he suspects his life is going the same way too. He has no need to suspect anything; His life is secure and thoroughly thorough. He's just pissed off that my life is more than his. I will tell you now for nothing that the only thing about my life that is more than Harold's is the lies I will tell him. I lie to him so he thinks I am more than the sum total of his piss poor pathetic existence. His life is shit, and so is mine; he has nothing to be concerned about.

This is me. This is what I do. I do it very badly. I know you agree. Throw me away, toss me in the bin you measly fucker. That is if we ever meet, which is unlikely. I'm doing this now because of Harold. It's because of that stupid old bastard sitting opposite me doing all his thinking. That and the girl. The Girl who. Yes the Girl who. That bird who. Who made me mad and angry. I am mad and angry now and then I am just angrily mad. Mad about it. Fucking fuming to make no too finer point about it. I am so mad and angry that Harold is mad and angry and he does not even know it. It's rubbed off on him. I ejaculated a whole load of shit life on him and now he's got that shit stinking same old hole of an existence also. My Father hates me using swear words so I will stop now. Like fuck I will. Actually I will stop the swearing. There's no place in literature for swearing so if it's literature you're looking for try your nearest charity shop. I have no idea why I said that. I didn't say it, I thought this as I scribbled over the page. I'm just doing to the page what has been done to me. By her. By the Girl.

That's it. That was a previous attempt. I feel more positive about this one. It's like this time it might actually work. I lost my way with it all. The main reason I decided to scrap it was because my Father peered over my shoulder one evening and said.

'I hope it's not full of foul language, this book your writing?'

'Of course not, it's a short story anyway.' I then saved my work and scrapped it. You can see for yourself why.

It's late now and I should be in bed. However great works do not produce themselves. They are created through blood and dedication. It's no two minute Pop ensemble we see adorning the streets with perfection. Perfection and genius, they are the creation of our home and the magnitude of our incapacity to comprehend the what, why and wherefore go I.

I am not crafting. I am pursuing. If I happen to catch my quarry at any moment just whisper yes to me. Let me know that this all means something. My great work of fiction here is the ticket out. The best part about writing this kind of literary prose is that all the hard work gets done by the critiques and the audience. You are my audience. I sprinkle little petal's for your audience. The hard work yes. I as the Author of this piece am not at liberty to tell audience what it all means. The answer is simply out of my hands.

I have nocturnal insanity. So do most of my friends. I wish I could cure them. I know I need to sleep now. I can't go on like this. I have to take control. There must be some structure. Structure is to a great work what routine is to autistic people.

There is something wrong with me. I slide away and straight through; I'm on a plain I wish I could hear Kurt Cobain say again. I loved myself I loved you too. Hey dude if you're still on that same plane wave when you pass over. The fucking religious festival of Pass Over. Pass Over. It's called the feast of Pass Over. It's Aliens that Pass Over and deliver aid to the people.

I hate myself and I want to die, wrote I.

I'm disconnected. It's too many years of being affected. I have lost my youth now although it hangs like an Albatross in legend of verse. I will quote ye. No I'll do it later when I'm more in the mood to. If it pleases Sires. I cower behind a lap top nervously doing okay in life, too terrified to talk over the phone at work. I am a living breathing mess. I don't even go out to pubs and clubs, a stay at home I can be.

There is a web site called Local Tart's and when you logout the banner reads as; thank you for using Local Tarts.

I just want to go now. I think about running away and starting a whole new life. It's just not realistic now. There are people whose life flies them away at some point to a world beyond their wildest dreams and the ladies who get to be among the rich and famous. My circumstances I feel are about to take a turn inwards if they have not done that already. I want to go now. It's a case of Sympathy for the Devil. I want to see your little Devil tattoo. I am too.

I am crying inside. Or so it seems. Little parts of me keep crumbling away. I was only joking about the Great Work of fiction. I was planning on with holding that piece of information until much, much later. You see now my Dears I have this great story to tell you all about. I might tell you. I might not. I either will or I won't. Like Holden Caulfield found out about living - You don't know what you'll do until you do it. I think he says something like that on the last page. If I don't finish this book then you will never know what it would have said on the last page. So take it from Holden and me. No one ever really fucks up their life because they wanted to.

With a few rare exceptions.

Tormented by the sound of road traffic shooting past the house day and most of the night. The lorries start rolling past and over the loose grate on the road directly in front of my bedroom window. And no woman gives me love. I am since the final departure of my wonderful and joyous mother utterly unloved by another; completely unlovable to me.

I'm just making all this up now of course. I don't have a clue what to write about. So I thought and remain to do so, think this. I contain an urge to sit for hours tapping away at a lap top keyboard. That's what I'm doing. I am completely obsessed by it. The sex on line. It has devoured my loving heart and replaced it with silicone sealant. It's a scam you're being ripped off. The images and stories that are circulated across the globe now filling our heads with glory, torment, anguish and love in all its greatest forms. Because the night belongs to life. I lay my head down and rest a while with you. I'm not the voice of God or indeed his Earthly Offspring. Spring, that's better. I am a tapper. I'm tapped by the hands of something Earthly or otherwise. Get this now, this is the fiction.

I don't hear the stories that circulate. I see the product of fiction as it seeps like a needle of blood back into our arid veins. There are many fictions and some are expensive and wasteful of Fossil Fuels. There are moments when life seems unreal and desire of wealth all too enticing. Actually that's not what I was going to say. Don't buy into that. Don't do it. You don't know what I speak of. The urban Legend. To be the Man and His big bitch.

My obsession. Tapping keys. What I try to get at is the question. It's the one about being tapped. What does tapped mean. Go look it up in a Dictionary if you're interested. Well since discovering like it's ever been a tale of two cities we are all tapped in our own special way. If that were it.

I have just written the last sentence of this good book I plan to write on the screen. I have also moved the cursor above this sentence so it will plop gently into place when I get to the end of it. If that ever happens.

It's the stories. They are the pollution. Its gossip gone mad. Gossip and viewing lives as they are now. So up to the moment we watch them sleep. Stories are just that, fiction. Stories like trains ploughing through a mind already unhinged by the pollution of tap water. Would you like your water with water there, sir? A waiter may one day exclaim. Synthetic water taps everywhere. As much as your silicone sealed body can hold of the synthetic digest. Take it anywhere you can. That stuff grows anywhere it does. That's water.

You're more likely transporting me further than I'm transporting you who move around a lot. People who have never read a book in their life. Granted intelligence is still present and must have a Kindle. To read. There's no turning back from the danger of on line or digital information stored. When that system crashes as we all know it will sooner or later. That crater of hot liquid is going to blow every parliament and other members of society groveling down into the mud again. Centuries devoted to getting out of the quagmire and all we have achieved is a few inches. That's Mankind's greatest accomplishment. We are all of us a whisper away from this. I have no word to name this collapse as. If there is one I don't know it. If this was to happen and knowledge is lost without hope of repair then there can be no reparation for any of us. The key to the knowledge that is vital in the event of global information loss. That's not a war. It's not even nuclear. It's big. There will be no party political broadcasts. We can all sit on the beaches collecting bottles and after reading the letters we add our own and place the cork back in the bottle. Watch it as it floats away and out to sea. The tall man sitting next to me on the beach removes a letter from one of the bottles and reads the fragments left intact.

Dear Mum and Dad,

                    I sent this letter to you because I want to let you know how much I love you.

The tall man beside me is now disintegrating the letter in the frothy surf at the oceans lip. He proceeds to pull another letter out of the bottle and reads.

Dear Mr. President of every fucking Country, Nation, Colony, town, or barn that's still.

The tall Man stops and starts to laugh. He cannot hold back. I was the President of the United States. That's about the only thing he states these days. It's something he cannot hold back from. He sits at the lip of Synthetica. The first great synthetic ocean. All day he sits and drools dying from starvation. At least once a day he finds a bottle with a letter that begins with: Dear President. He actually was the last President of the United States. Can you actually believe that I am sat next to him on that beach now? No of course not. If I were I would leave him to his own devices.

I suppose I should tell you where I do live then. For the sake of accuracy I live here, there and everywhere. Armchair traveler, that's me. Why I do it I don't know. To just sit in front of a laptop screen night after night for years. What does he watch I wonder? I watch the letters appear on the screen. I have done this recently more and more often. I actually quite like it now. It feels like it's becoming easier for me to explain the story to you. This great work of fiction I hold in my cerebral domain has to be told as it befits my certainty of its success.

A dream.
'I can't stop it,' she said, pausing to take a drag on her cigarette. 'I'm sorry.' the lady coughed a bit from cigarette fumes, 'now leave.' So I did leave, almost at once. She could not stop what she was doing any more than I can. Who can just pull over into a lay by and change drivers if there isn't a lay by to pull into. She couldn't do it. That is she could not change?

## The Watchman

That's a part of the story. So legend has it.

It began to sink in with most people when clocks became unreliable. The way the people would remove measurements of time and surrender to the organism. That was what we all hoped for then as much as we do today. The organism will provide us with the vital staples to continue our survival. It's not harsh for the later generations. It will be all they have ever known. The regression might be brutally aggressive, so are the abilities required for adaption.

Earth to earth, ashes to ashes. The great work of fiction. A life time's achievement buried beneath the ruination of our capitol. Who would buy a book on such a day and then find time to read it? It's there to be read.

I wonder if there are any great works that rely purely on audio recording. It's just that with narration it's such a task to fit the pieces together seamlessly. I'm not making myself clear.

I can't focus anymore. My personal situation just blows between my ears. I'm desperate; I am desperate enough to be aware of it and also to let others know in a matter of fact manner. I can hardly breathe. This life takes my breath away. It's Saturday night and all I can put together of my feeling is forgotten. I'm on my mind only and others are glad to not have me on theirs. They all think it's her. It's actually me. Me, so down I'm practically buried already. What am I talking about? Its okay you don't have to answer that. It's not working anymore. Nothing is working. That's for the best. There has been no one single person I ever heard yell about fixing any of it. There are for sure plenty of peeps out there who would know and choose to keep shtum. We build a path to destruction, it's a garden we keep and we must never forget. This garden and I are one. We are manure. We are a part of the cycle. There is no end. There is forever changes. We are manure for tomorrow's peeps.

This is a lonely and isolated path. All I can imagine is how to get off. I can't imagine how it would be possible now. Tonight I do not have a friend or lover on this planet. I am alone. Abandoned and befriended by every one other than a lover or a friend.

I want to tell you this. Tell you all about it. I would show you if I could. We both know that's no longer possible. How are we ever going to pass on all the fragments of knowledge enough to inform and later rely upon them to know what's going on. How will they know? How they shall know.

All I would do with my life is write one book and hopefully it will be good and then I shall die.

That what you have just read now was the last sentence of the Great Work of Fiction. As yet there is no new last line. I will be sure to let you know when there is one.

**Woman**

Oh I won't
Pick one thing
It won't cost
I don't cost
And I pay my own way.

Where are you now
Never ending stranger.
You went without a sound
Across the years.
Where are you now elemental stranger?
Who passed through walls
Without a fear.

Where are you now beautiful stranger?
Who took my hand without a tear.

Don't know what that was all about. You could call it compulsion. To write things down. To keep a record of moods. I can be very funny when in the frame of mind to be such. I always end up writing misery.

It's frustrating me to not have a last line. What if something was to happen to me before my book got finished?

I've been so busy fussing about last lines and words, too far gone. That's it I'm done. No more that I could add to this now. I've not actually told you the entire story yet. In fact I have barely begun. It's very much like I want my book here to be great and fictional a lot more than I wish for it to be work. I may die at the last line sat slumped at my writing desk. The thing is this: it really wouldn't trouble me if it was only to take twenty minutes to complete. I'm beginning to think the whole wham, bam, thank you great work of fiction is going to be work. Work is something I have genuinely spent most of my middle aged life avoiding in many varied and splendid ways. Great work they will all say with jealous smiles held with fishhooks in each corner of their mouths. I shall savour that moment standing before a huge hall filled with literary types giving me a standing ovation with fishhooks in the corner of their mouths, hating the living day lights out of me while I feel the hate, pure and green hatred raining in psychic showers down on me. I smile and absorb the energy so easily mistaken for praise. We praise the Lord; we do not praise one another. It's a genetic thing. Not being able to value another above and beyond our selves.

I have now made the first line of this book the new last line. It's already been cut and pasted directly beneath the curser. I left the Full Stop in place as evidence that it was an earlier last line I had demoted to the first.

It's just this minute dawned on me that was a stupid thing to do. How could anybody take me seriously now? I'm playing with the text like it was all mine to toy with.

I'm not doing very well at telling you the story. It's most likely a Novella. The plot is quite simple. It's all about a man called Fred who is working through the night as a night watchman. Hence the title. Now this man Fred is working. Ah now if you read the out take text I decided to include you will know most of this already. So for those of you that skipped the out taken text. The story so far:

- Fred is a man in his late fifties
- He works as a security guard at a weapons plant in the middle of nowhere.
- He likes to be thorough
- He likes to think a lot
- He is thinking a lot about life and where he lives
- I'm not inclined or decided where he lives at this juncture.
- He works with a young man who passes the time writing poetry.
- That is me
- We don't talk much
- It's about the inner workings of Fred's mind
- I know a lot about Fred
- He's wondering what his wife is doing
- He cannot get back to the city until morning
- You could say it's doing his head in
- It's doing my head in.

So there you have it. The story so far.

I can and shall tell you more of the story when the time is right. The right time is not now. There are more pressing concerns on my mind at the moment. It's getting too much for me and I am unable to cope. It being the internet. It's unbearable. I sit and wait for messages from people I don't know and will never meet. The only interesting thing in my email is the spam.

Did you know one of the problems with my mental condition is lack of inhibitions and poor insight? Well anyway that means nothing really. It's the lack of motivation and being so gullible that gets to me the most. I get ripped off by everyone and do you know what? I always know I'm being taken for a ride in some way. I just go along for the ride. The thing is curiosity and that's what always gets me. I want to know what you want and why you want it.

So what. So what do you want from me? I can offer you zero. Not a thing can I as Author say about this. I tickle the type writer and she laughs and says argh you're tickling me.

No one likes me. I dread the day my Children will realise this. That moment is years off and already I feel utterly humiliated about my social status. I am many things and here are just a few of them. I am: a berk, weak, weak willed, small cock, big penis, a numb nut, a sex pest.

For reasons of interest I might even give you my contact details. Now challenge my intentions. Take I for a ride and at least make it interesting. That, dear Reader, is my best of intentions. I say this evening I have been contemplating a rather sticky end. Drowning is all I can reveal. Its murder I feel; death of self-confirmed. Death in deed. Death in deed. I speak with my tongue in cheek. It's death of a kind. It's the end of being one of a kind. The herald of which blew doom across the lands for all us slaves.

Would you like a sneaky peek at the last line of my great work?

The watchman - sputtered I

There you go! Seen it.....

Go say I. Look away from the awfulness of my story yet to be told. Fred / George, has pangs to return to his home. He should have. His wife is apparently carrying on with another. It breaks my heart. It really does. You see now Fred isn't so innocent himself. He knows this and so does his bint. That's why she carries on with them.

Would anybody really hold it against her? I would.

I feel the need to be communicating at all times these days. When I am at work or alone I have to either be sending or receiving text messages, emails, checking emails, social networking sites, talking or just playing spank the monkey.

The Watchman

## Status report on the Author of this Great Work of Fiction

Author is a savvy gentleman at heart and on the surface of things he continues to maintain an appearance as such. Over recent years The Author has become a dark heart of lust. He has been in training is his only explanation for his covert behaviour. Despite his claim of complete open honesty we have no idea about the nature of his dark heart carry on. The Author maintains that he conceals nothing. I live with mortal fear of being caught in the act.

The Author wishes to remain anonymous for the duration of his great work, he shall however release an identity profile of himself when his great work is recognised as such or upon his death. For the time being the Author shall continue to use a pseudonym. His preferred name is Guy Wilgress Hudson.

Guy Wilgress Hudson can be very amusing at times and has been known to make people laugh to the point of becoming unconscious. It would seem that this ability is not under any control by the Author. It manifests spontaneously during times of mild psychosis. The Author has been in varying degrees of psychosis for a number of years now and he states that it's been happening for such a long time that even at its peak the Author remains to all purposes an average person to a casual observer. The Author is plagued by sexual urges he has no possible means to fulfill.

End.

I have another last line. I can talk about that later. I will leave it hanging like a suspended sentence. I have a book to write. They don't just write themselves you know. I'm going to bed now; good night everyone.

I'm making very slow progress with this story now. I am finding it very hard to keep off the porn. It must be one of those difficult patches you hear successful writers talking about. They tend to say at about thirty thousand words you hit a wall. This is now seven thousand words or there about. I can't go on like this. I'm hardly even making an effort to type in the story. In fact most of my time is divided (unevenly) between sniggering at internet porn and writing. I think the Author has lost his way again. I think I should employ a lady to write the actual body of the Great Work of Fiction. She would have to understand the Authors wishes and exactly what the main intentions of the Author are in the writing of the body of the text.

I have a feeling that if I can keep this up for another seventy thousand words I really might have something.

Seventy thousand words. Imagine if you can holding this book and reading off this page the very words that I am typing now. Keep reading for another seventy thousand words. Words are one thing that are not affected by inflation. Words are mighty and weighty subjects. I am amused that the later it gets I feel less inclined to go to bed and sleep.

I regret it all now. It feels very much like we have passed the point of no return. I must either begin a fresh and tell you the story or continue writing on this page and risk not getting the flaming thing told before I finish. I know we are only just at the beginning of the book but look how soon and excessively the Author has deviated from the writer's path. It's absolutely essential the writer tell the audience everything that's needed to be told before the Author finishes the book.

I watch Fred as I scribble furiously on the blank report papers. He has an extremely vacant stare for a person who wouldn't experiment with illegal drugs. He's thinking again. Thinking he is and that's what he does. All fucking night long. It's just not masculine to do so much thinking Fred is what I try to tell him. They lock you up in a cell one of these days and leave you there until your through with it Fred. He doesn't care or even hear me sending agitated annoyance at his thoughts. You can take your Dollar with you and you can't take your thoughts with you.

This is a thought of Fred's: That the season of spring freezes over right in the middle of all the new shoots coming through. Things freeze and remain that way. He reckons it will happen one day soon with no warning. The only precursor to the catastrophic event will be the rain beforehand. It will have rained consistently for a considerable length of time before ensuring everywhere is coated in water.

So everywhere is frozen and none can alter that. We simply wake up one spring morning to find ourselves shrouded in a world of ice.

I am lost again. Telling stories is a tricky business. I lost her. She left me for another man. The situation is appalling to me. I will never love again after that relationship. She didn't make a fool out of me I did that all by myself.

I think that's enough about the Author for now. Let's not forget this is fiction. If we are able to say everything we want to then we don't have a lot to say. I think people say too much. Silence is the measure of true friendship. My eye has gone into a spasm from staring too closely at the screen. It's either the Porn or this desperate last ditch attempt at proving myself capable of being more than bad at everything. Either way my eyes are in spasm when I attempt to concentrate on the matter in hand.

I need a new last line. I can't cope without one. It's something to aim for. A place in a finite space and time. A last line that shines a guiding line on the course of the story. I will attempt to come up with one now.

Slightly more important than a last line is the feeling I have today that I must disengage with internet adult dating sites. That's something else I need to talk to you all about. I don't know why you need to hear it; I just have to tell it. Let me tell you what I did last night. My girlfriend was about to go down and rim my arse and I got all self-conscious and grabbed a piece of tissue and quickly wiped it just as she was about to make contact with my rim. It made us laugh. I felt embarrassed. Then it was really very funny. You should have been there.

I'm not actually telling you the story am I, what a moron I can be.

I have had an idea. I'm going to begin again. So I will begin again at the beginning. Here is the new last line.

The Author has no intention. The author is not at liberty to critique the work. The Author has no voice. If the voice is right it don't matter what's been said.

Phew thankfully I am back from the new beginning. Its ok I don't expect you to go back to the beginning to read what I have just written. You might know the beginning already. I'm being silly now of course you know how this begins. For that matter you already know how the great work will end. I shall underline the ending for you now. I might do some editing of the last lines at some point.

I think I may have peaked a bit too soon. We need a time and a place.

Here he is now. All you need to do is turn the page.

# THE MATCH MAN

By Guy Wilgress Hudson

She writes in time to
This far gone tune

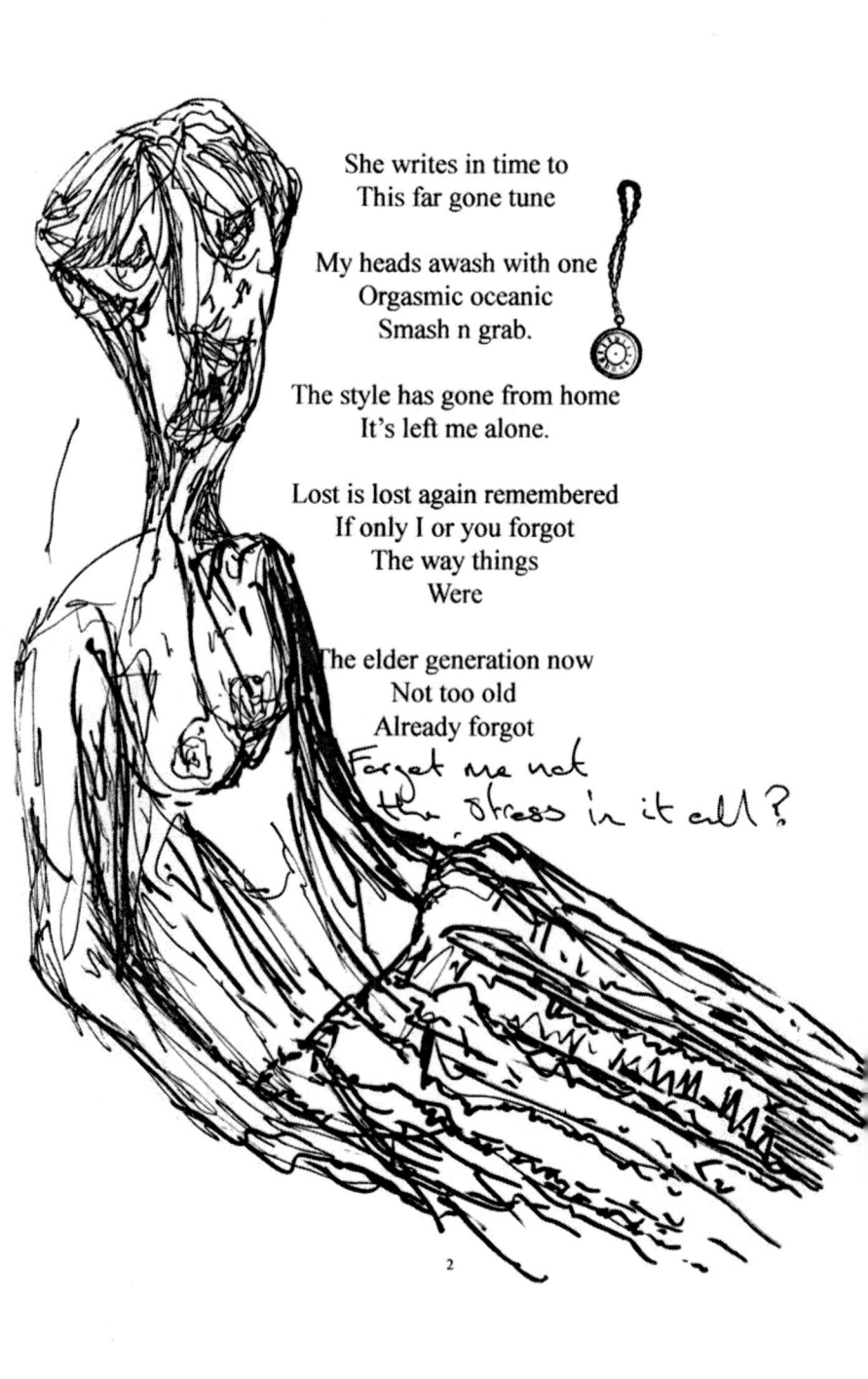

My heads awash with one
Orgasmic oceanic
Smash n grab.

The style has gone from home
It's left me alone.

Lost is lost again remembered
If only I or you forgot
The way things
Were

The elder generation now
Not too old
Already forgot

Forget me not
the stress in it all?

Now I'm so very lonely
Now nobody will
Own me

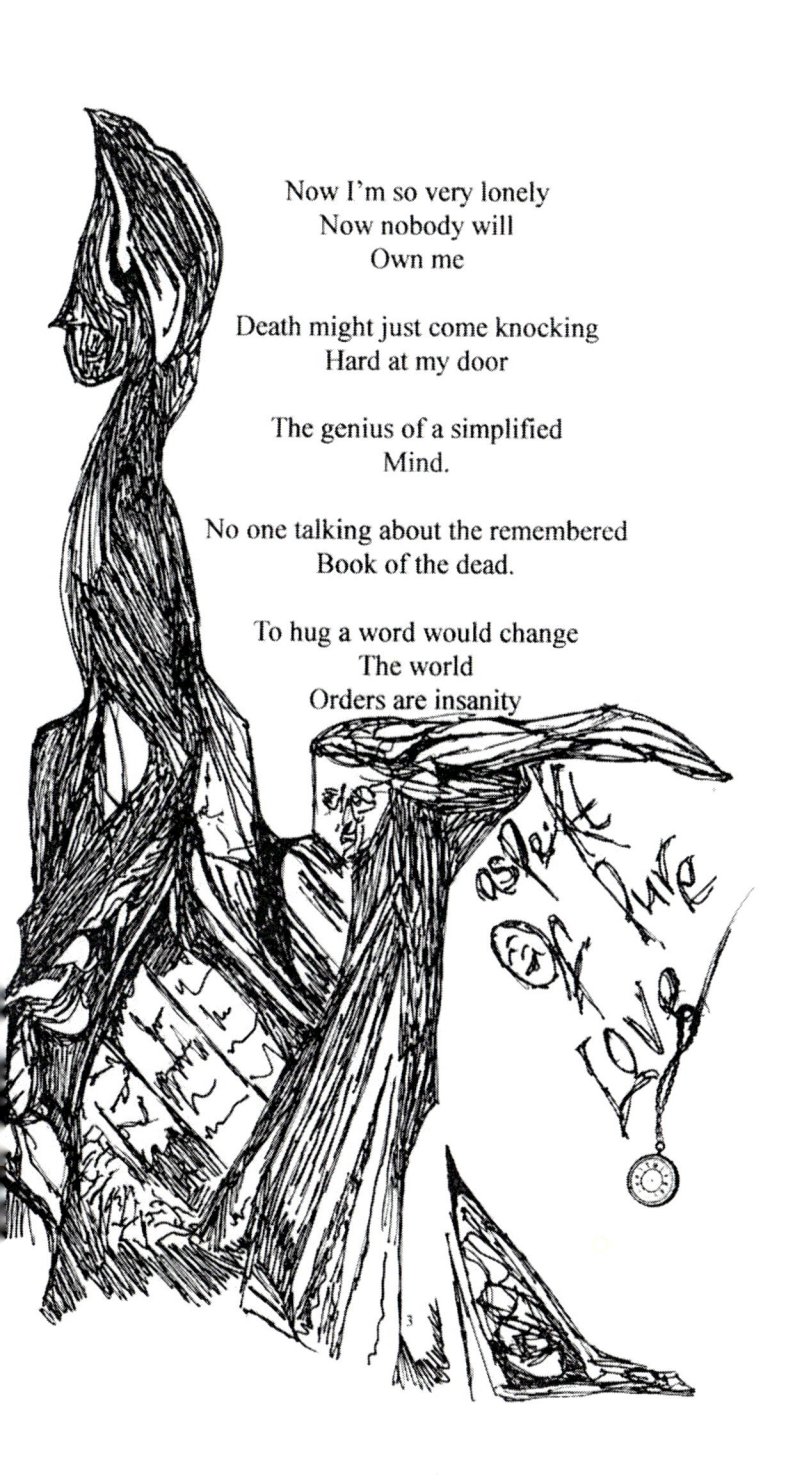

Death might just come knocking
Hard at my door

The genius of a simplified
Mind.

No one talking about the remembered
Book of the dead.

To hug a word would change
The world
Orders are insanity

The trouble is there's always
Some trouble

Going on whatever you are
Trouble is the agoraphobic
Mind

Unparalleled they wont ever
Meet.

I cant wake up, its not aloud.

To dream of peace in a war torn
World.

I haven't had that.

## Paradise revisited
## His fortune regained

Renew now refresh
Funky patterns
From the pen
Earth bound
Life now
Seems to have no end.

Sonnets in a sextet
Signings in a doorway
Whore way church.

Change your name

Earth bond
So sound
Then change it again.

Go back and fill in some blanks
Different voices
So sound recorded.

Plopping made by rain
Hitting the puddle of mud.

Independence day
Alien and symbolic
New York, New York.

Independence day
American way

Everyman make haste
For himself.

The greater foe
Us alone.

Chicken

I spent twenty years working
    On humiliation

The movie was hyperbole
    To soften the blow
    Of this real ordeal.

    Such nonsense
Cannot be ever known

I love that broken gate

I see the bombs fall in Greenland

Helps keep the water fresh

Tundra ice sculpture

Canadian wolves

Bison not safe

Wolves in the wood

The fire on earth
The battle resumes

Not oil to burn
Water to quench

There is a long way to go

Freak zone

Oh I don't understand this

It's so bloody late again

Just sit and do nothing

You tell me

When it all went wrong

Since there was no one
Really out there!

Crashed again

You can't turn on

Its getting late now

I know what you mean.

I didn't speak to anyone

Its bad bloody awful

I'm a slave to the show

# Liberty Leaves This and

Freak rules

Don't go to bed in a muddle

If you are in a muddle
Best go to bed.

Stay up until your calm again

If you've become calm

Don't smoke weed

Don't throw the weed away

You may need it later.

Be negative

Negative and optimistic
Make a present of the future

A mole is always that way
Inclined
With Pandora.

I think I will get the sack

And return to the driving
Cruise.

To see clearly
Has been
One to avoid.

Good and bad artists
Have one thing in common
They are misunderstood.

I haven't played you in a while

My Trumpet too

We have not long enough
To play U2.

Your not a patch on anybody

Your some kind of patch
To me.

The fire keeps burning
As the year turns

Hot in a flash like

The flickers of a faulty
Tube starter.

The winter heats too cold
To care

Diogenes flew in from a window
As the Eliot Ladies

Come and go
In the room

Where Tea and cake
Was an equal

In the case of the bird.

It were off again by morning

Defer all meaningless
Activity

Until further notice

Porn on the walls again

Churns in the urn when

All at once my Pizza

Troubles me yet again

Leave me be in my big
Reality

All we learn in lots of science.

Nails grip her to the wall

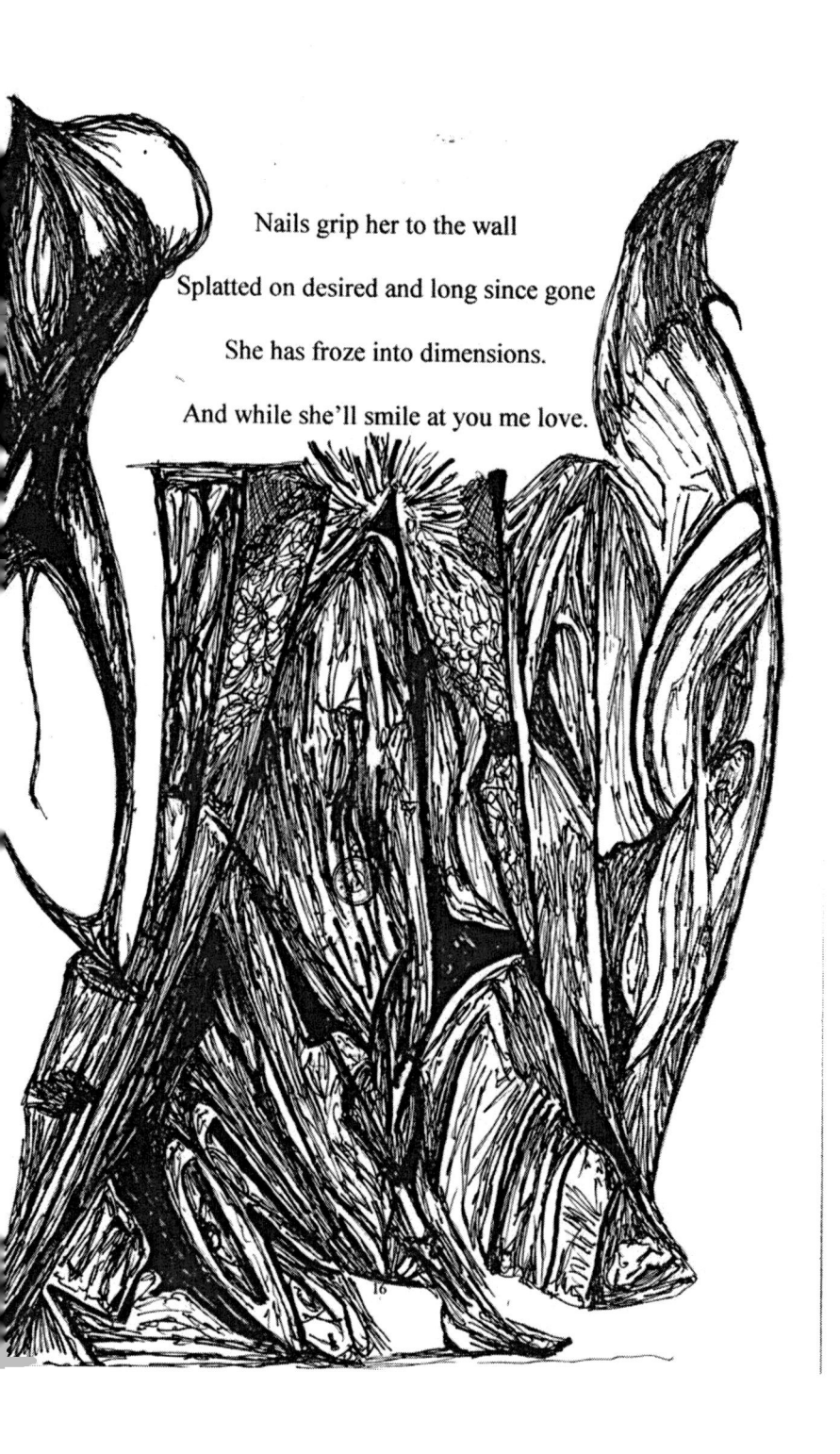

Splatted on desired and long since gone

She has froze into dimensions.

And while she'll smile at you me love.

Desolate house you could be anywhere

In the world the wind wisped around

And gathers the sound

Of a whistle

Between bad teeth.

What can I be what I be
Is how to be.

Yet to be stars

Gas giants awoke me

Said an ebullient beast

Morbid, infantile and desolate

Yet to be devotion

For the toil and pleasure

Measure the pleasure

Toil through the day.

He's better than me

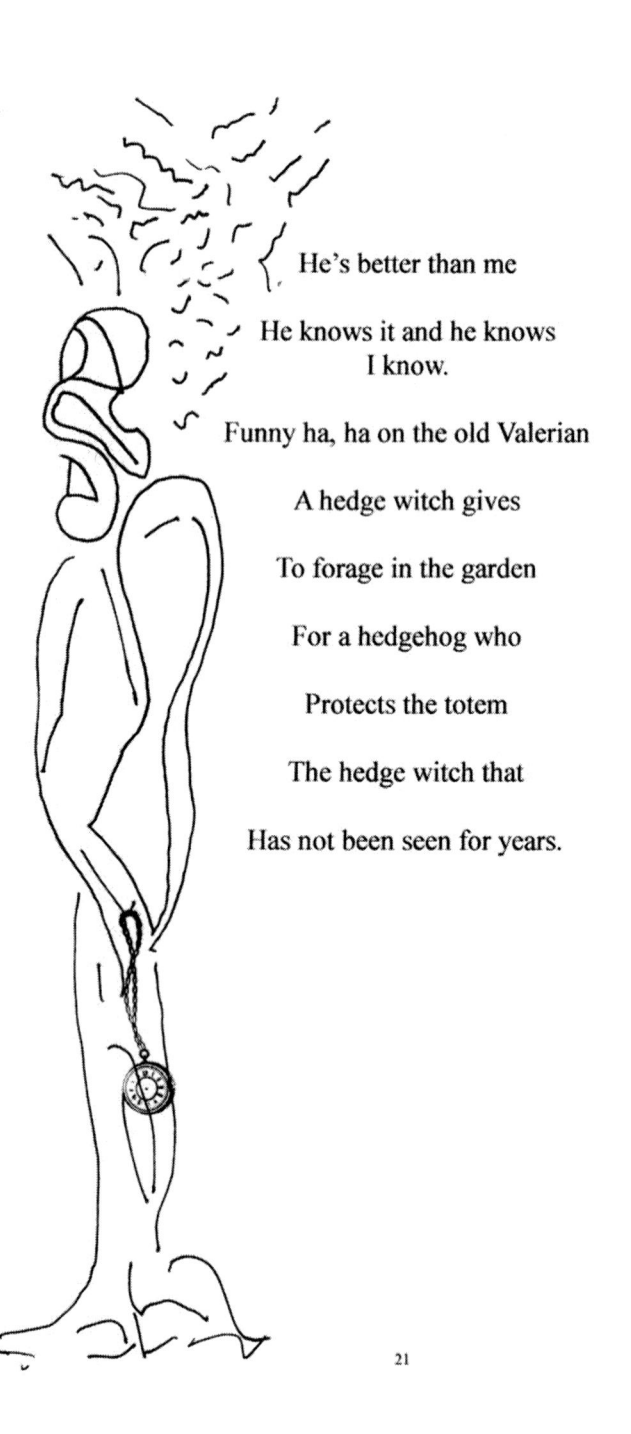

He knows it and he knows
I know.

Funny ha, ha on the old Valerian

A hedge witch gives

To forage in the garden

For a hedgehog who

Protects the totem

The hedge witch that

Has not been seen for years.

# The Watchman Takes no Prisoners

Oh no! not again
Yet again I'm afraid to say

There is no gain in economics

No matter how home economics
Failed to fill me full
Of domestic bliss.

The sturdy fat cats on the midnight
Trail

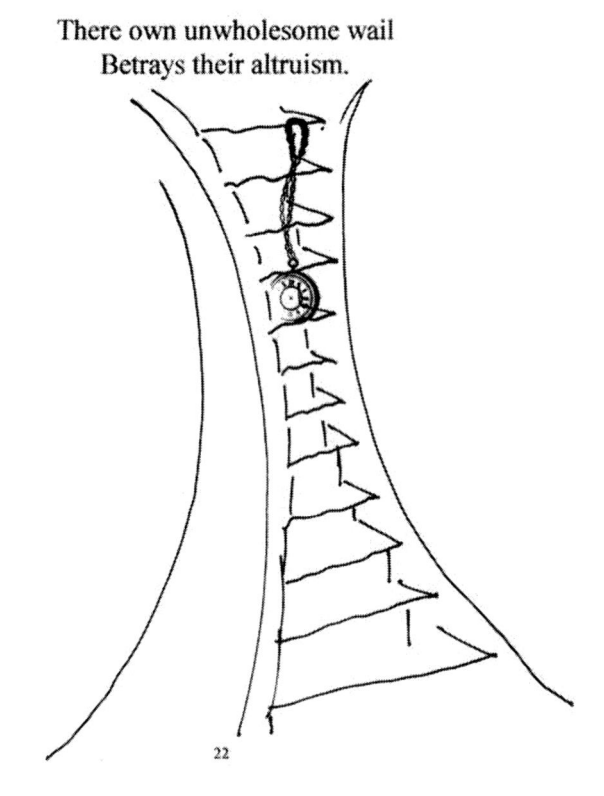

There own unwholesome wail
Betrays their altruism.

Who celebrates record profits

My prophet tell me

This is not good

Do they need to gain

Year on year

To celebrate success

On a business account

That chomp at unrivalled

Magnitude.

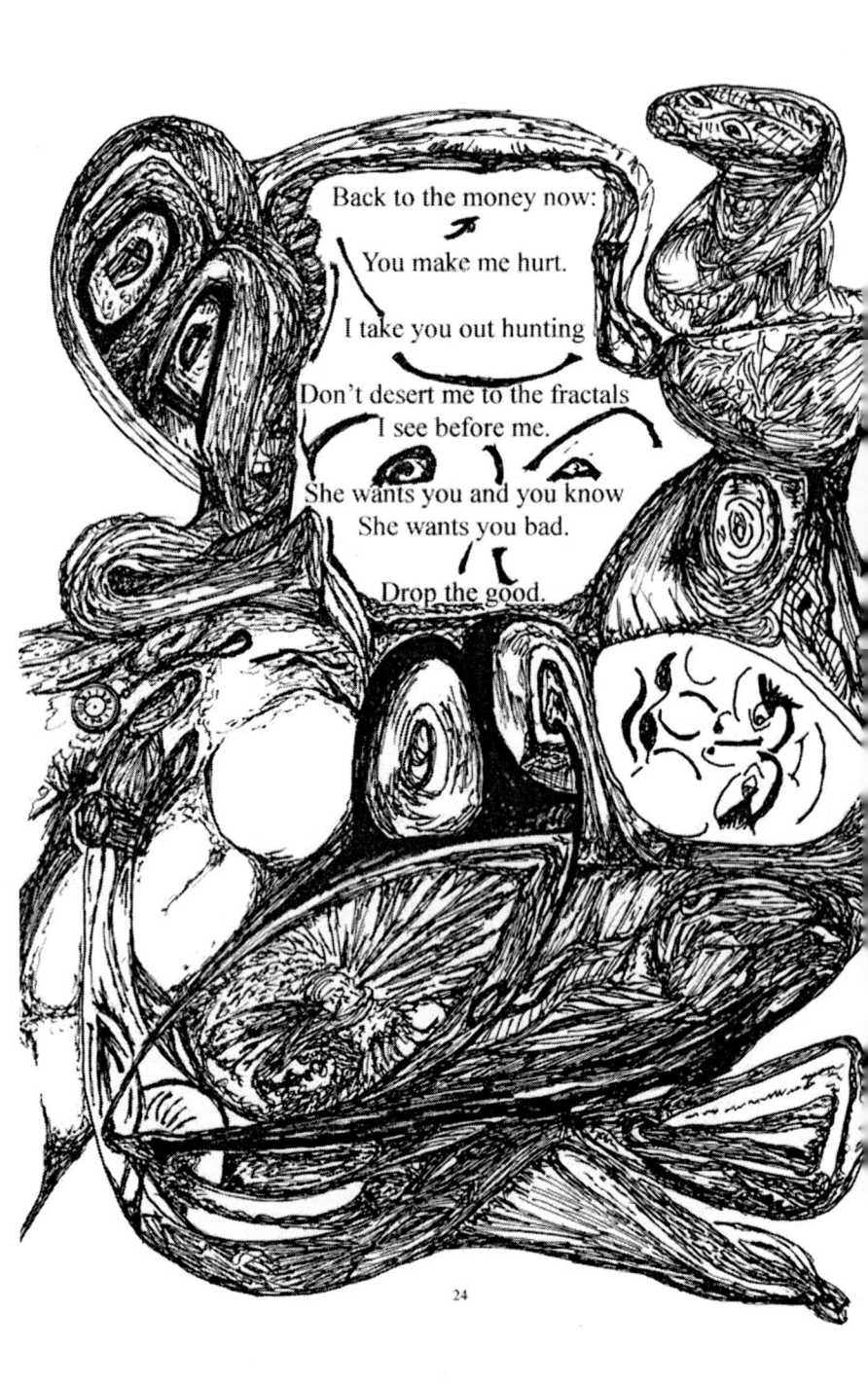

Back to the money now:

You make me hurt.

I take you out hunting

Don't desert me to the fractals
I see before me.

She wants you and you know
She wants you bad.

Drop the good.

I don't want to meet you

In an internet chat room

I tell you how hot I am

A fireman's plot

He knows what the sun must have

And he knows he knows
No more.

Dear Doctor, me, me, me!

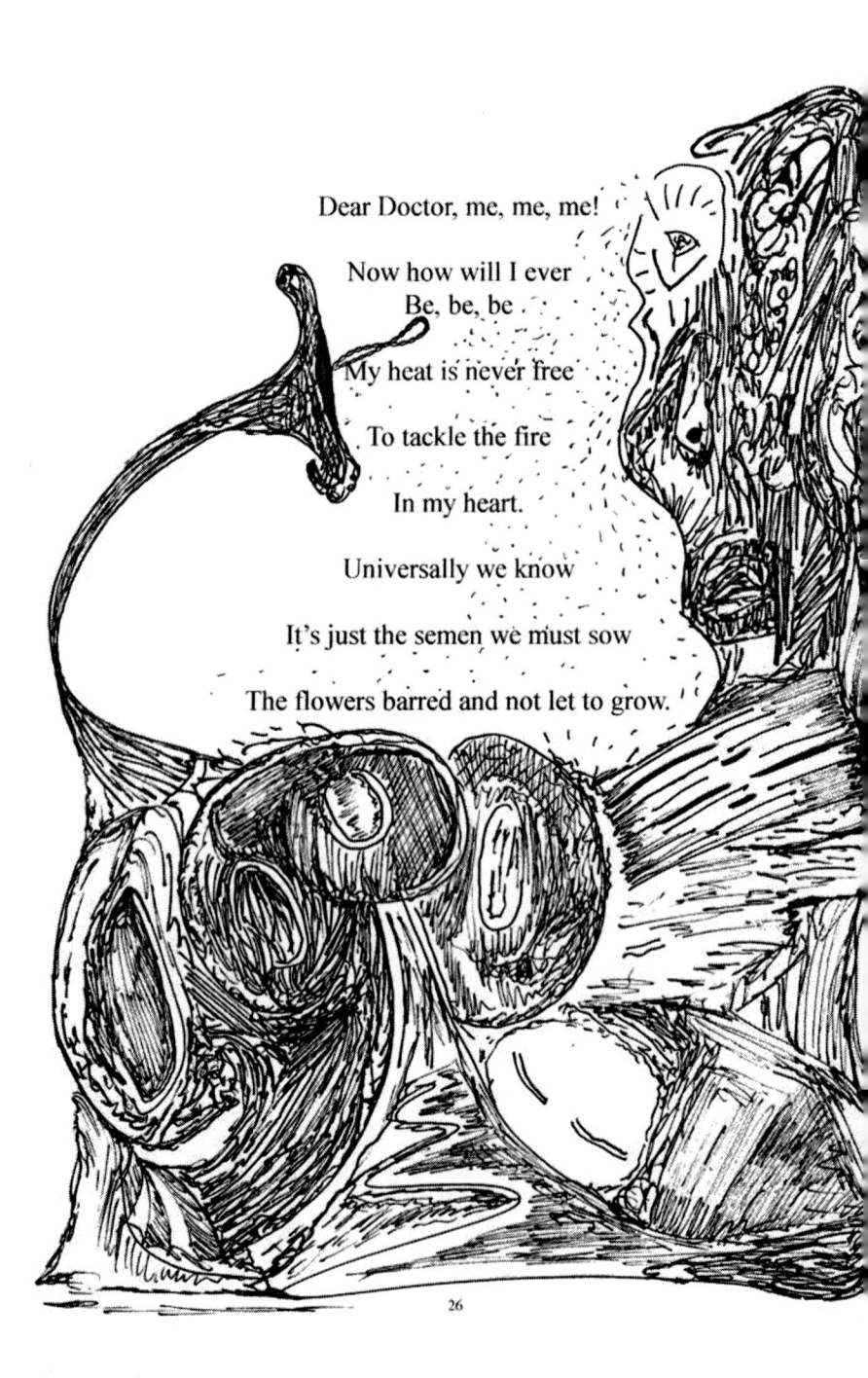

Now how will I ever
Be, be, be

My heat is never free

To tackle the fire

In my heart.

Universally we know

It's just the semen we must sow

The flowers barred and not let to grow.

Spunk in my hand

Cum into a heart

Never the same so always apart.

Co-joined at the hip

On this similar trip

It must be the jiz we all know

Burns Babylon, burning

On an ego.

The bottom line.

*am unable to define my form.*

Page fillers aside

It was no comfortable ride

If you wont live

Your never going to die.

If you should pass

Then beside you a shrine

You made me cry

Now no body listens

Who could guess why.

*Inside a hail storm.*

*I don't know what I am any more*

It was supposed to be about
War

The righteous battalions collide

On either side before grace

Hero's are mad and damp

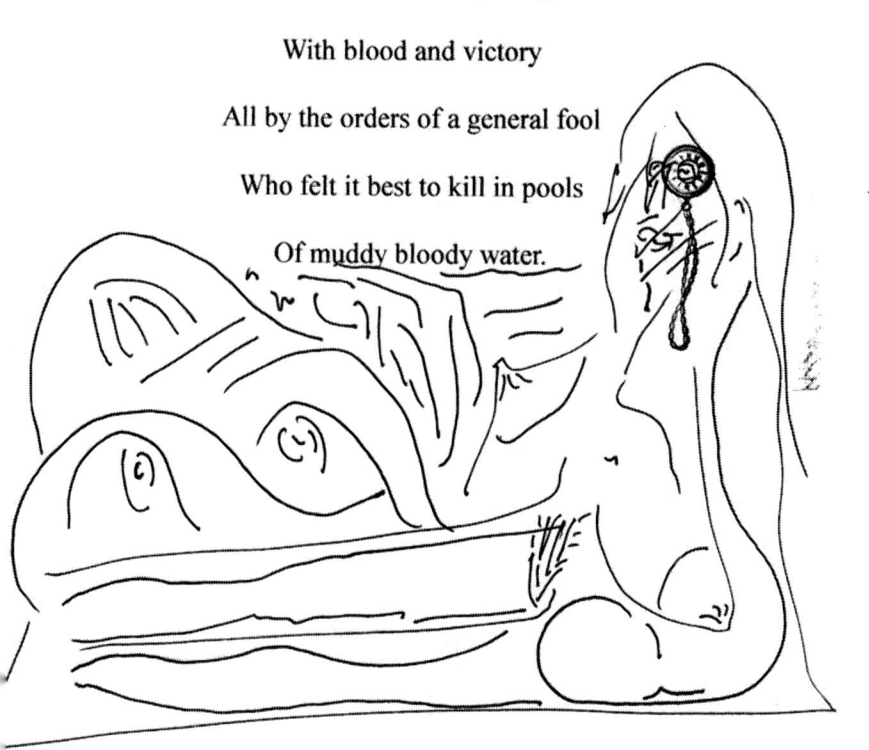

With blood and victory

All by the orders of a general fool

Who felt it best to kill in pools

Of muddy bloody water.

Those poor bastards to the slaughter

I would only for a wife and daughter

Not ever on the order

A general tosser

Who plunders

Our mother and hungry

Brother

Drags us bleeding

Through the mud.

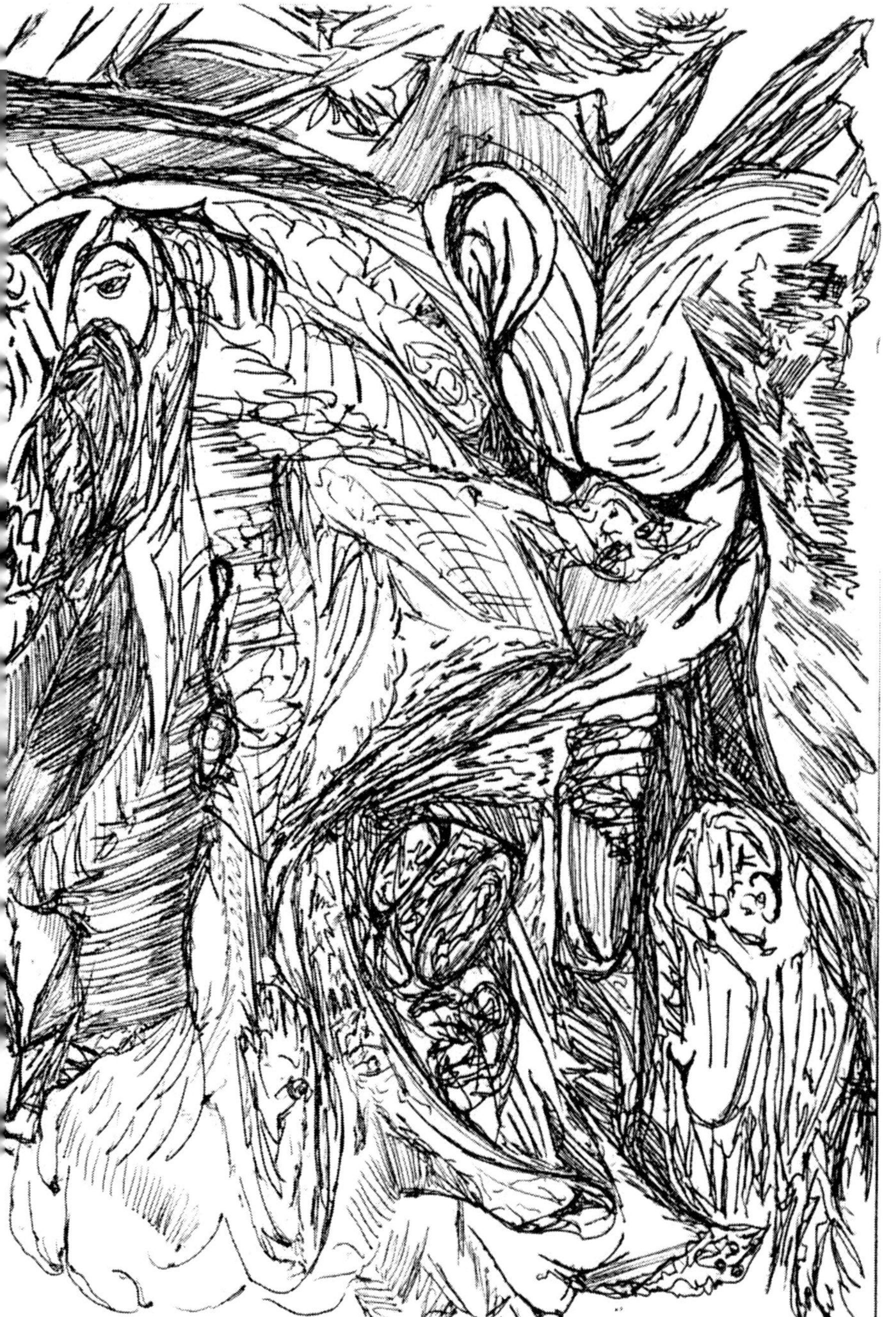

I know I am just sick
Of the dicks who come
Thinking the answer is cuts!
I would answer your profit
As a gross indecency.
The corporate few celebrate
The fact they have fleeced me again
And I should applaud their industry.

I don't like their profit

Their profit is my loss.

She wont text me
She wont call

I saw her talk to me as she set out her stall

Over the wall

To the cabbage patch

Such a great fall

For a little lady spider

Waiting for a delicate spider

Who wont come

She wont stall

She bears a light of innocence

That I cant take at all.

I smell a rat in that

So sorry about the unit
But it rhymes.

Could anyone wear a brighter image
As youth.

Step into my lair if you dare

To take a chance and extract some juice

From these grapes and grind them.

Travel the world

Distribute freely

As a bomb of love

Stacked against hate.

This is an anti-human march
Movement.

The exact nature has been lost again

My myth of past and future

Remains penned inside my brain.

Who can tell now all is abuse.

Who will listen to the loser

Of the first degree.

That is matter what got gathered
In the university

Life did abase me and turned her weeping

Back to the day before
Christmas.

When Santa prepared his full sack.

You turned your back
And Smirked.

If I were to ignore her now

She might go astray.

The myth of Santa lasts

Not much longer than a day.

Sitting here all alone

Feeling stoned and enthroned

If backstabber were here

I would know it in my inner ear.

The truth is yes the truth hurts

When I was a child I saw a film

A role I grew into with ease.

Happy that she will be happy now.

So sad I wont be with her to share it.

Minds been made up and it's over.

Last night I could have cried.

I just don't think about it now.

You are so special through and threw

I did love you

In that respect I was always true

Although I cheated

Again, again, again

These substitutes for love

Were what kept me going

Through the barrowed land

Of your love for me ending

# The Watchman approach

I am just trying a new pen

Bought as a gift for a lady.

She didn't get it

As she didn't want it

And she's not joking either

When she says

Friends for ever and for ever
Amen.

You turn me fool in love

Lady to make me wise

I can fail and free fall

Now I read the writing on the wall.

Shall I fight for her return?

She's so long, long gone

I don't know her at all

She came back to me

To say goodbye.

All there was vanished

In the blink of an eye

For here words are turned red.

In and out of the same old bed

At different ends of the day

Is all it took to destroy us.

After having vowed to never leave

You weaved a fair web

In a fever departed.

You gave me liberation

A freedom so far unknown

You broke in and broke me out.

Out to life once more with adventure.

To work and toil and party.

All this benefit without effort

So easy you won't ever know.

Without her I would be dead.

A second chance has been taken already

So much so failure is not an option.

It's all now gone beyond the pail

That is how I failed.

So set on world domination

I think I forgot you were there

A long time ago

I see you more as an apparition.

It was a function of survival

That I took for granted

She can go and be happy now without me.

We used to hold hands

Always and forever

Now I forget when that ended.

I can't recall the feeling

Of our hands together

I lost us in my pursuit

Of happiness.

I let you down when I should
Have picked you up.

It's a mystery why things get done
That way.

After so much sadness

I hope you can be happy now.

I want him to be
All the things you want

That I wasn't

And will never be hopefully.

It's one of those days

Not to blow your own Trumpet.

Believe me I tried to

And could hardly get a note.

To achieve nothing

Requires effort

And demands

That people like us are riddled
With surprises.

All of life is on show.

I picked up a chick

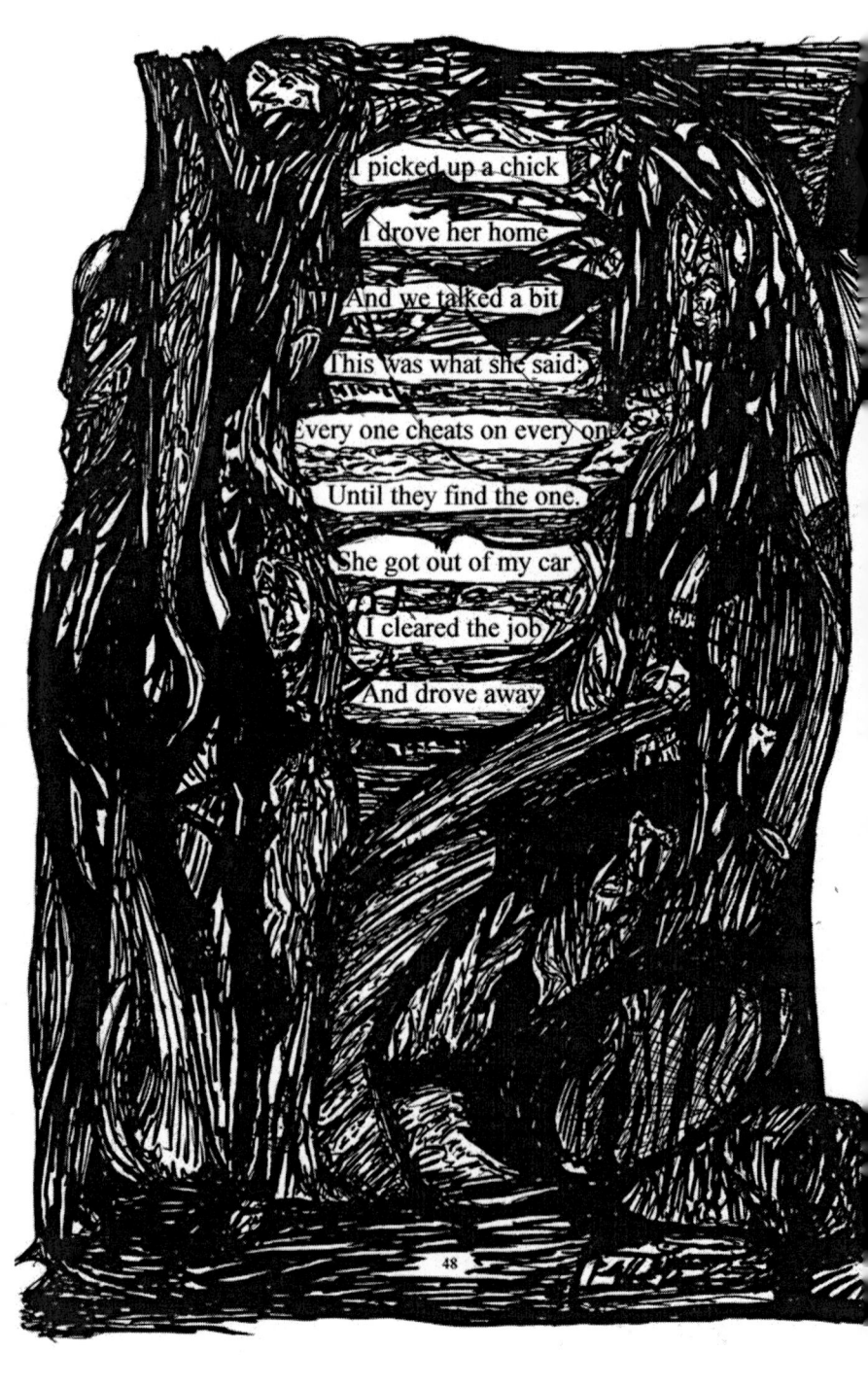

I drove her home

And we talked a bit

This was what she said:

Every one cheats on every one

Until they find the one.

She got out of my car

I cleared the job

And drove away

She was ugly and stupid.

Cruel to a highest degree.

Butchered in a moment

When rejoice was on my tongue.

She took it away

Okay it's now today

I am so far gone from remorse

It no longer seems impertinent

Now slander my seed and break
My heart upon your sleeve.

That it was longed for

Desired in every way

To take the fall

Bereft of all

The things we didn't say.

Since the war ended

I have been some what suspended

Rescinded and slightly deranged.

Christ, that bunch

Are fucking me right off.

If ya gonna take de piss

Feel free cuz you will me
The essential

that's which is essentially me.

Your words tore me.

Responsibility is where now

I set my children free

That's what I have done

They will come back.

Into my arms

Come falling

Look what you've done

You've ruined your sanity boyo.

You took her and fucked her

When I wanted her back.

What a gent you were

As you look right through me.

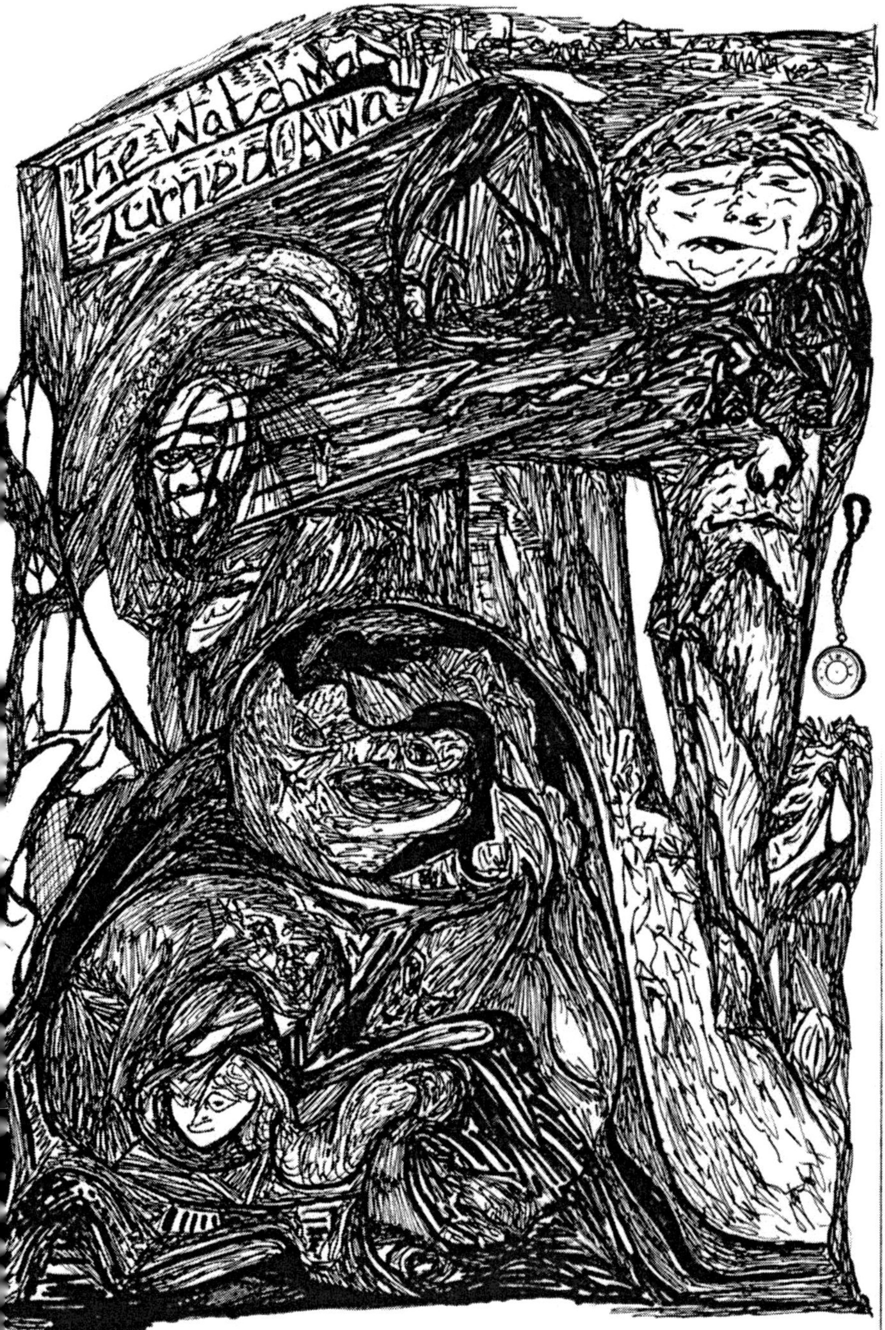
The WatchMa
Turned Awa

I handed you my wife

Who assured me you were
Happily single.

You bastard.

I had a whore in the house

On more than one occasion.

She made a dash with the cash

On more than one occasion.

Now I am a bastard of the high degree.

Something for me
Something for you
There is always
Something
for those who
live high on the
(hill).

You are a river of Scorpio emotion

So you and so alternate too.

Its such a quiet place now
The children are gone.

I fought hard for the right to appear
Foolish.

Not smart enough to pull it off.

To walk away before the fight

Seems to be fair enough.

It is such a dark and dismal night.

I know by the lashings of rain

Against the window.

This night is the night

I return home no more.

Home is now abolished
And abandoned.

It will be no more should I return.

The last kiss good bye

No more, or more, again.

This is the end of the night.

The wild wind whips and tugs
At my trousers

Like a new woman looking
For love.

The storm out there

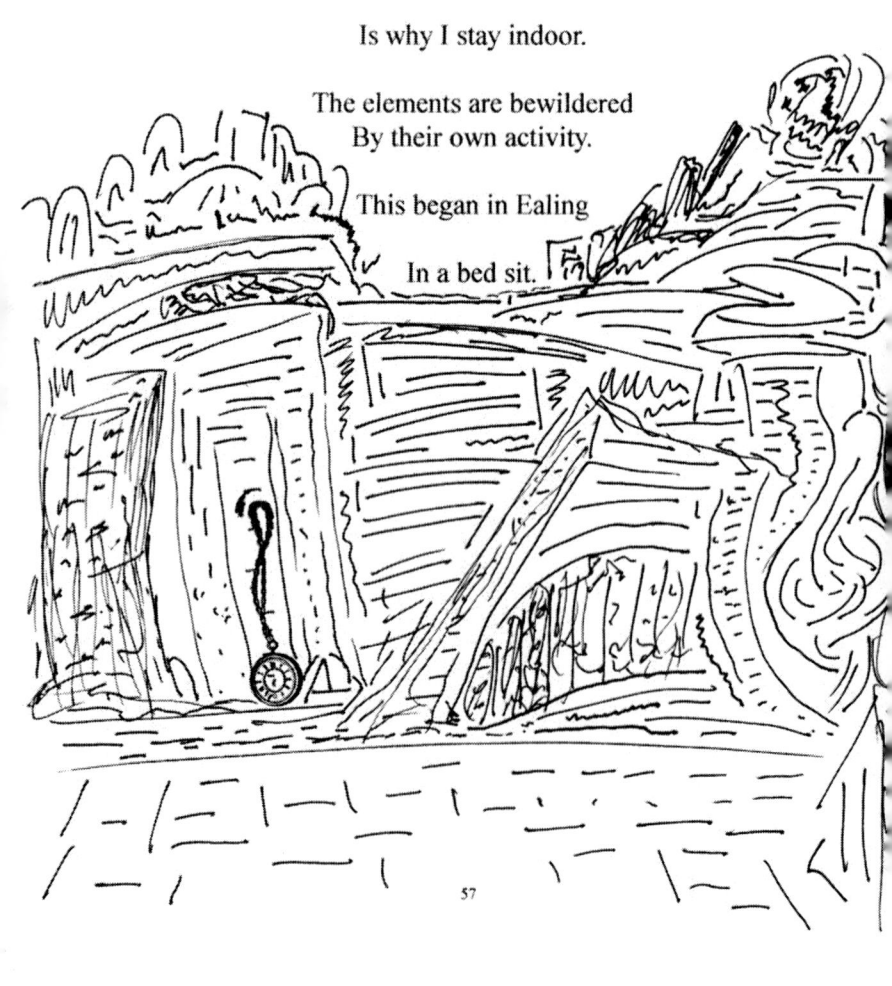

Is why I stay indoor.

The elements are bewildered
By their own activity.

This began in Ealing

In a bed sit.

Its been a while

And there is no money
For the whore.

So I text you instead.

That's a thing I should not
Have said.

that's all the thanks you will get

Everyone's drunk
Yet no body laughs.

I could friend request him on face book

Do I know him?

Not even have to search.

Do I?

I could chop off his hands

For the sake of you who understand.

The children are leaving home

At a very tender age

Its made me so mad

I cant help but shout

Because they cry

Because they know

There no more than a few days
Left to go.

thank you friend of my family.

A profound thought

I feel the need to document.

It's forgotten and in the past now

Oh, yes profound forgetfulness

Holds me centred

And tense with anxiety

That forgotten things
Are superfluous.

Never the master

Always learning.

I told that old man

Not all change is progress

The old grey matter informed me

Progress comes always

With invention.

Kind Watchman

I told him I want to fix and not throw away.

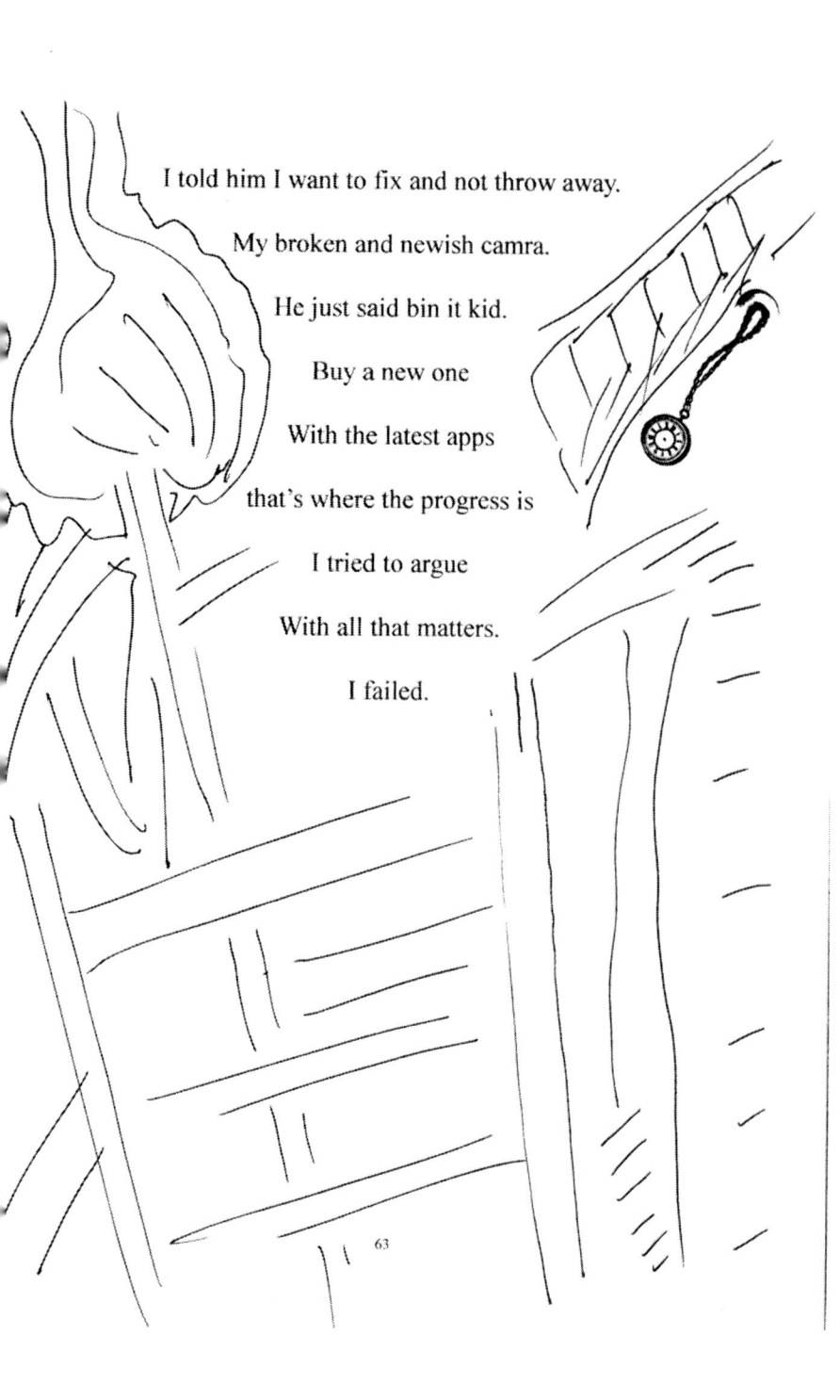

My broken and newish camra.

He just said bin it kid.

Buy a new one

With the latest apps

that's where the progress is

I tried to argue

With all that matters.

I failed.

Progress is in the eye of the beholder.

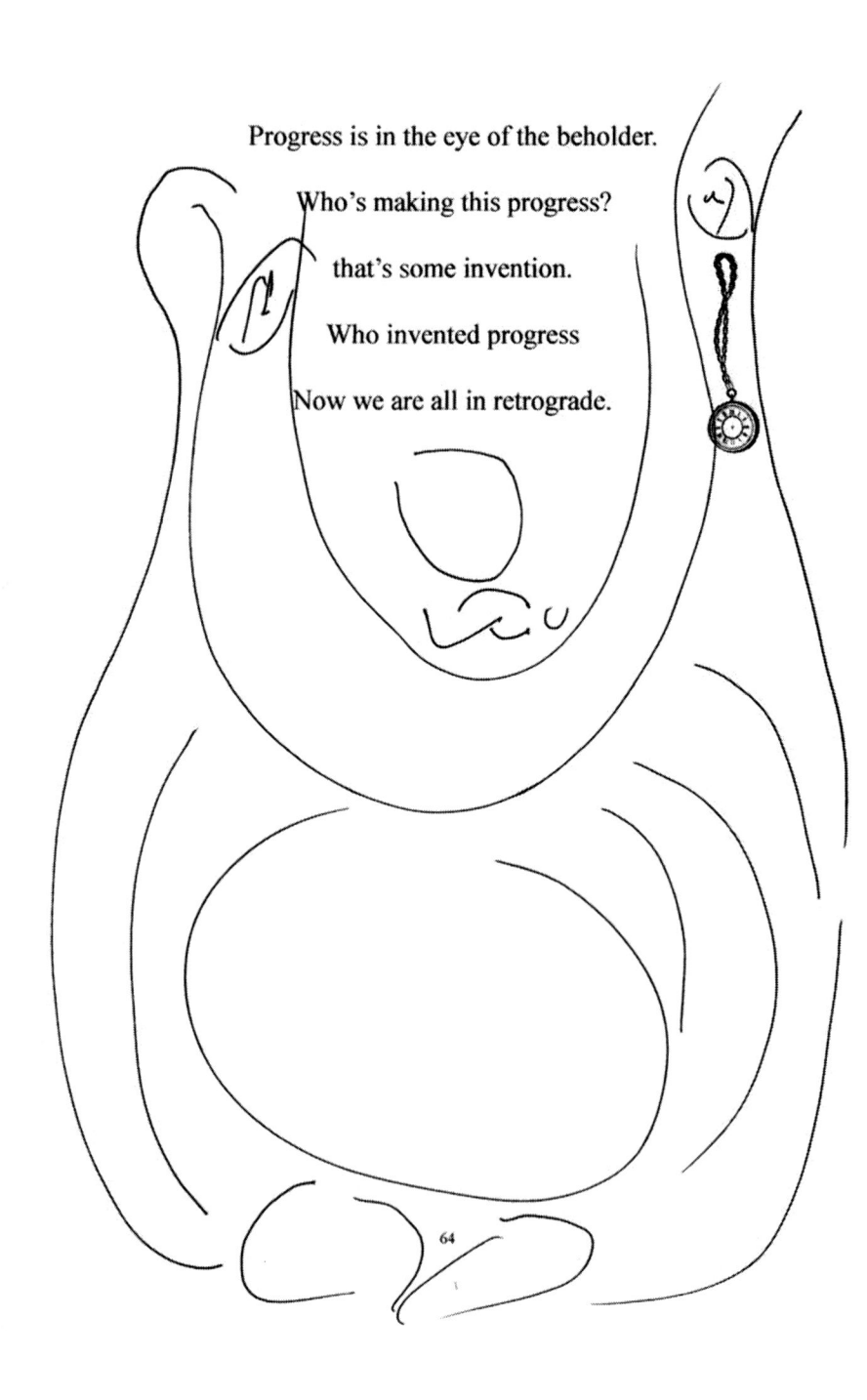

Who's making this progress?

that's some invention.

Who invented progress

Now we are all in retrograde.

# Knots

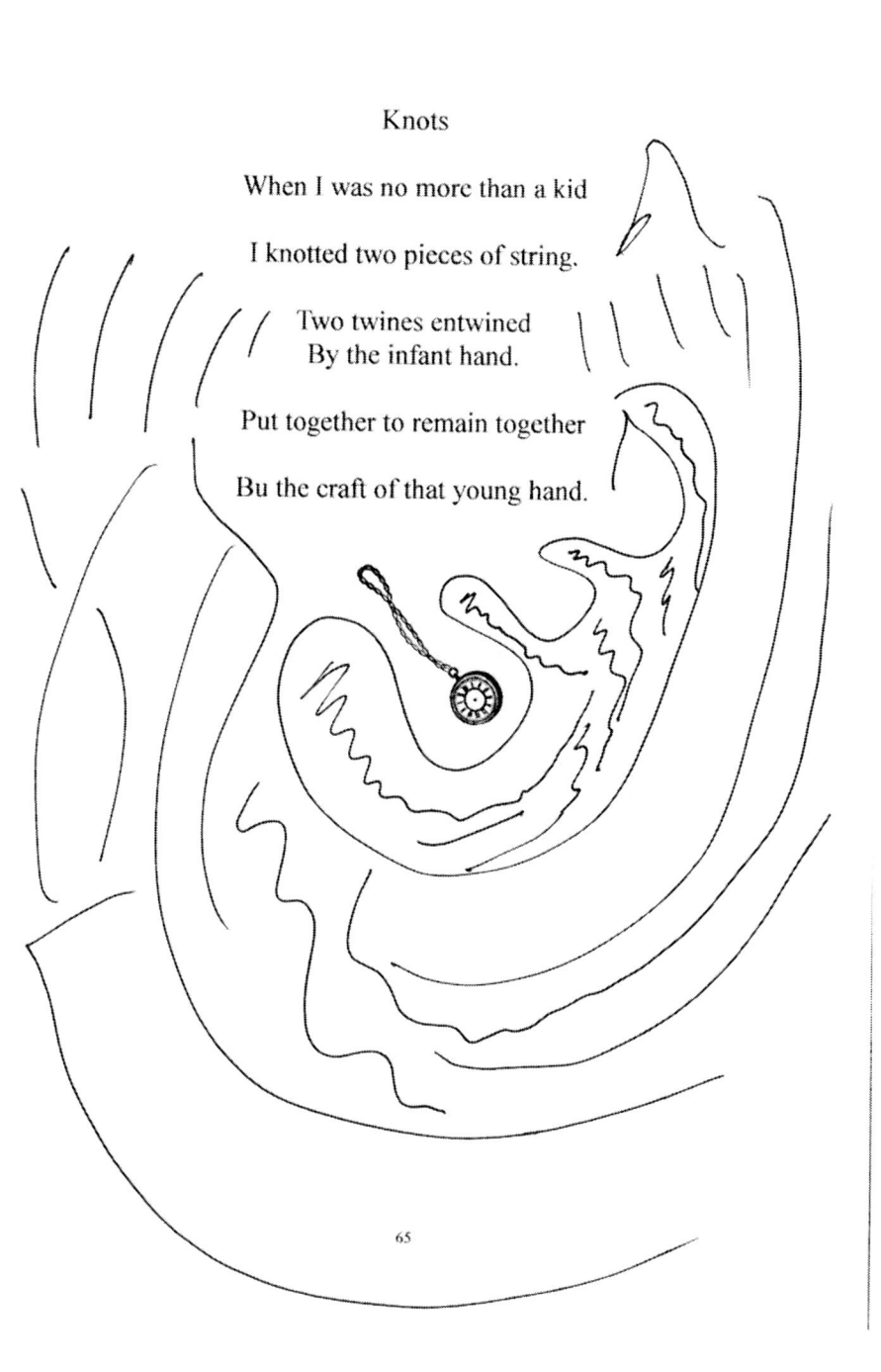

When I was no more than a kid

I knotted two pieces of string.

Two twines entwined
By the infant hand.

Put together to remain together

Bu the craft of that young hand.

The hands and feet looped
And bound.

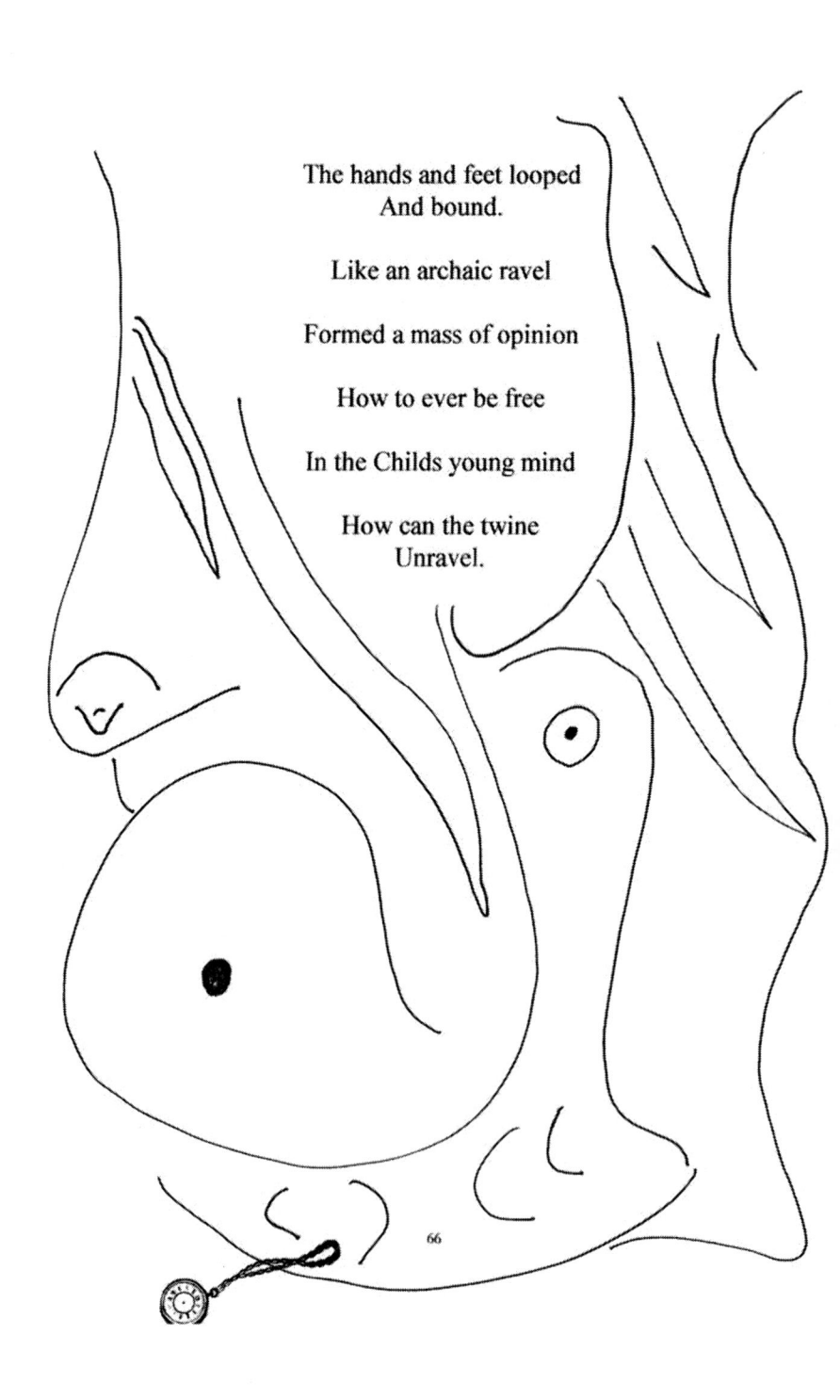

Like an archaic ravel

Formed a mass of opinion

How to ever be free

In the Childs young mind

How can the twine
Unravel.

To hell with him she thought to herself

Even I could do better than that.

A calm morning written in lamp light.

Are there no co joined phrases
In this phrase book.

The word was perfect

That fell from the voice of Him

Warts un all.

The flawed voice of God said
Alls well below

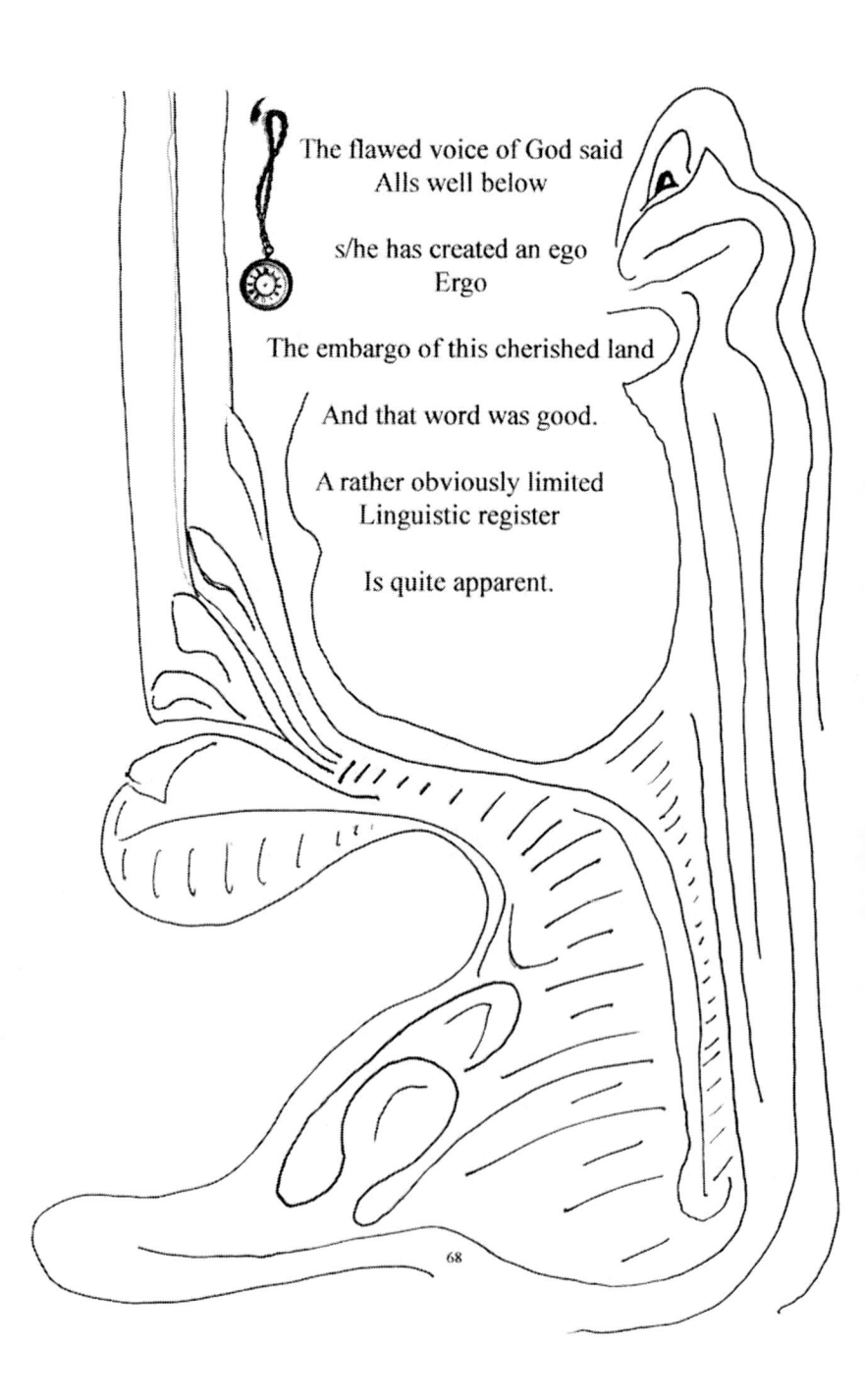

s/he has created an ego
Ergo

The embargo of this cherished land

And that word was good.

A rather obviously limited
Linguistic register

Is quite apparent.

The Watchman can Decide Now

Thus in an image

We were crafted

By his busy hand rendered

As above so below.

Mass production of man.

As man fell did He fall

The likeness is uncanny

With a choice un all.

Mirror, mirror

Watch me fall.

One night I ran the miles

To knock on your door

You were gone is what the rents told me.

To love and loose

A fever of the temples

Return to the Doctor

Perhaps he shall prescribe

Now.

Some quality leisure medication

It's a fine thing to outstay your welcome

When the world just slipped away.

Love it yes but still fidgety.

The harder the come the harder they fall

In good Gods image

Man began to fall

And His almighty semen

Bought creation to us all.

When He came he came the hardest of all.

...A defeated wreck of a God.

Where I have been

There has been no plan

All I have seen

Swells in the ocean

Of been and not been.

We thought ourselves as earth

To all of Gods children

We crossed the transparent lie

To the cities

We most want to escape from.

Last night he was there

I should have climbed the stairs

He was there he was.

He was naked in my underwear.

What did he do there

Why he played with the underwear

While the wife lady…

I send message upon message

SOS please take me in.

All I need is a friend said I

There was enough room at the inn.

She passed from friend to foe
My friend.

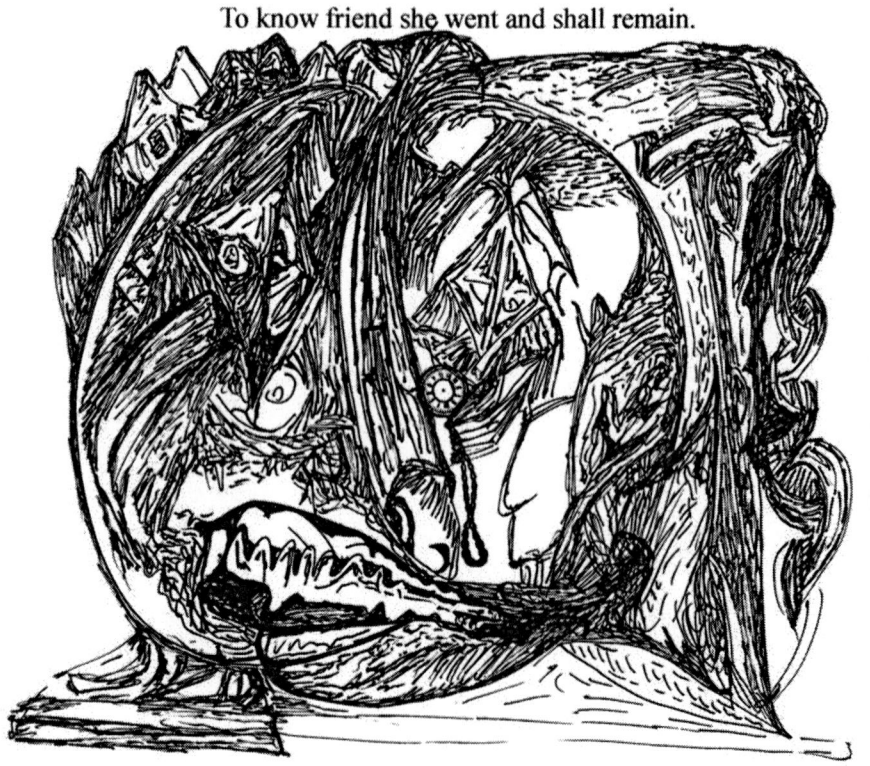

To know friend she went and shall remain.

Be now like all my friends

Take this unreliable narrator

Who has feeling

Without feeling anyone for comfort

No one loves the man

Who lost his song in all seriousness.

Revolt against your love

Is all those actions were

Pure and driven like a snow.

It was time to go

When the ideal home exhibition

Lost all inhibition

For a man with more than one name.

Now we are separate

I can finally strip you down to nothing

Unravel you without interest

In what had occurred

When we weed in the snow

You let your heart show

Me nothing in the end.

I always knew you had your secret heart

Stowed away safe and secret.

Intuition of which there is much

Told me you would be departing

And you wouldn't stay in touch.

These words have left you to it.

This love destroyed a part of you

Now with your chance renew it

Take hold of happiness

Leave your minds to play

You loved me said daisy

She loved me not every day

There are too many suns setting now

To take a glance beyond and beside myself.

The elements have given forth a choice once more.

Their tolerance is beyond our comprehension.

She failed to perform a function.

The function failed with it.

Surrogates were sort, met and managed

Devoid of emptiness.

# Liberty Crossing

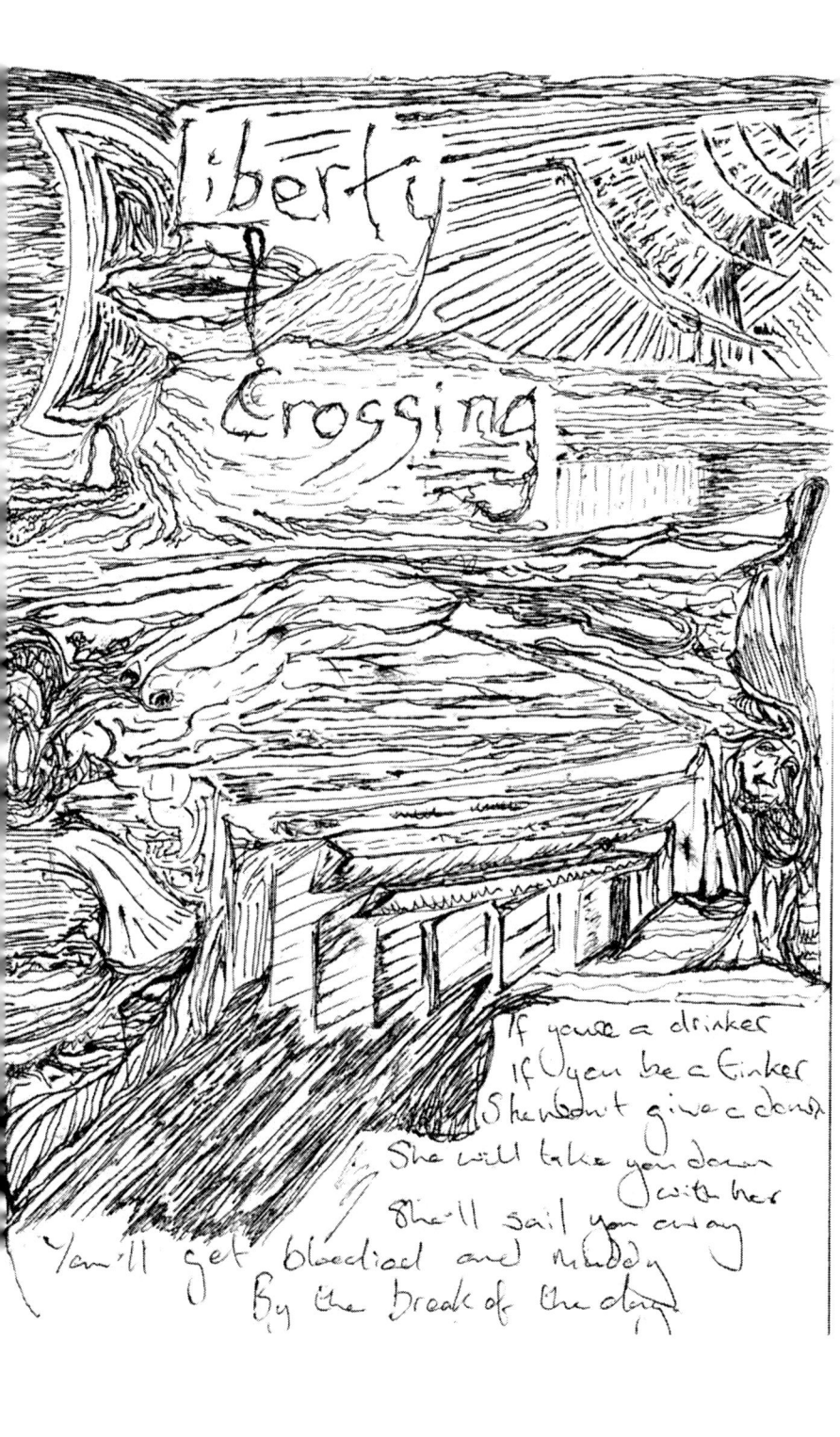

If you're a drinker
If you be a tinker
She won't give a donut
She will take you down
with her
She'll sail you away
You'll get bloodied and muddy
By the break of the day

Sides to take are irrelevant.

The separation for those inclined to know

Happened in a friendly fashion

So many months ago

I fail to recall exactly when

She drove me to the door

Now as never before

My feet could not touch the floor

For a fear of falling.

The world is watching

The ego here now driven to adversity

    You go on the high road

    I will pass down below

    If the calculations are right.

    Your on ya own now kid

    Better get working for thy self.

Silliness rose high those roof beams.

    Laughter filled the flow.

    All ways one day to be over

    One day your eyes will show

    Me how your feeling

    And then you let me go.

*A Monumental Testament To, Monumental Monuments. And the Torments of their Creation. The carver of creation Had no eye For detail. Preferring Black and White Too blind to see in the Spectrum of Light.*

I have seen you
Before in a
Psychotic vision.
Now you return
And still I do not
Fear

Some people have a condition

They respond contrary

To yourselves.

Insults shall be left at the gate

Hello my love, hello, farewell

And goodbye.

In front of you they whisper
Silent West never cry
My never did poor frankview
He will surley tell
you why. Unlike the I.

Now I wont go anywhere

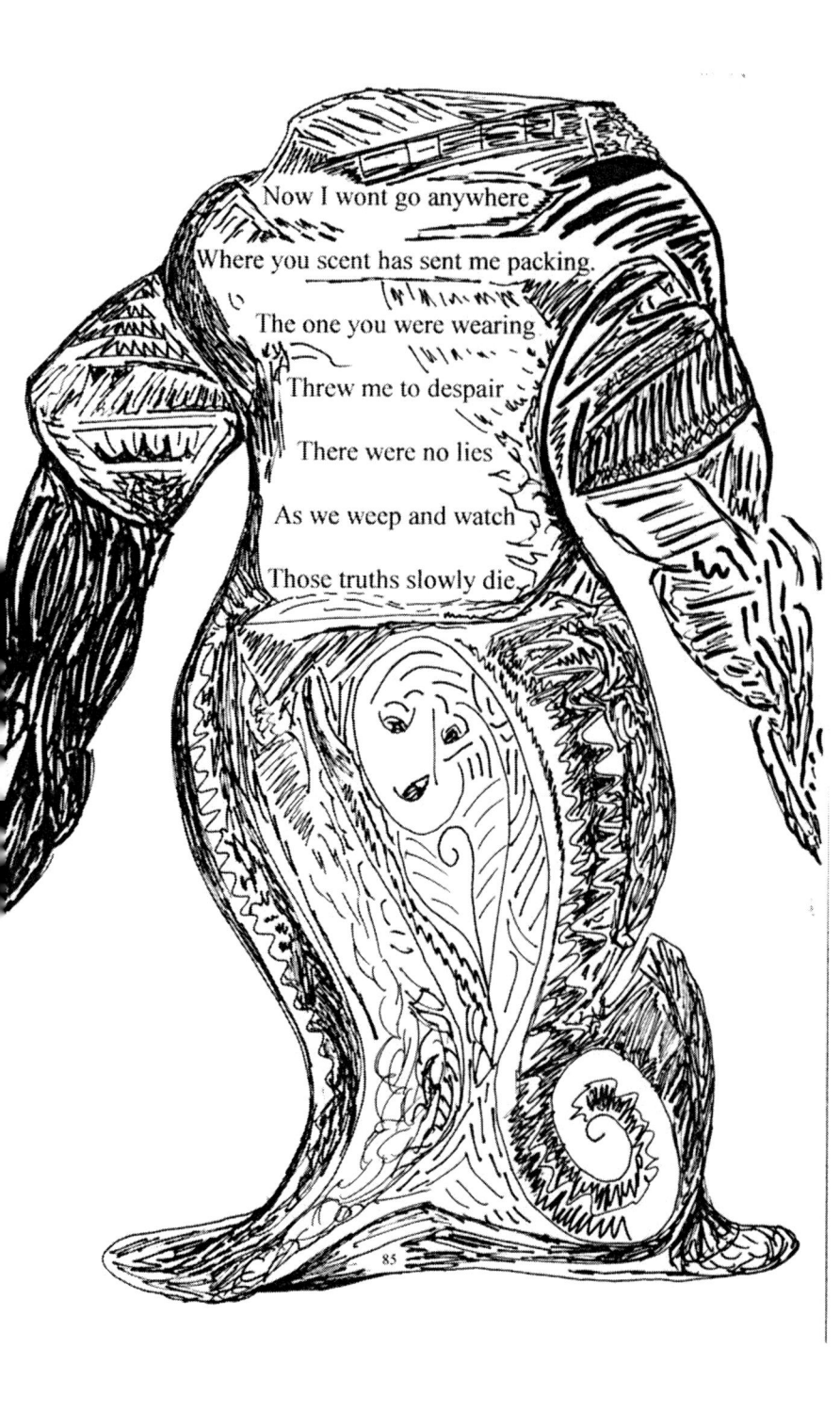

Where you scent has sent me packing.

The one you were wearing

Threw me to despair

There were no lies

As we weep and watch

Those truths slowly die.

The revenge you took no wonder was sweet

In these horrid defeats

Where love is a crime

Punishable by refusal of

That love is the very thing.

You are really the shadow of the girl

You once took in.

I never knew her

Who are you was the question

On the tip of the tongue

Of the eyes that were watching

You slowly move your self in

Before an invitation.

It was not even exciting.

Not an adventure

As it should have been.

Just another crappy flat

With rubbish jobs

No where to go but an empty pub

Where everyone stands alone

In the heart of a city

We have both to call home.

That you were order me do your bidding

Do your bidding no more

You wont catch me walk through the door

Once again

Nor ever no every no more.

& this
river
flow.

It's very cold out there it is on here too

Without a home and no means of comfort

So get down to time to know

Don't ever think its time to leave her

Time will say when its time to go.

The dawn light heralds bad news

Unfaithful once more to an unloving muse

There are seven seas for you

You are one when no one cared.

It's a remarkable life

Looking back on it.

Before the sharp edge of reality

Threw off the gauntlet

The challenge cast to keep all faithful

They have no love now one and all

Not even sympathy

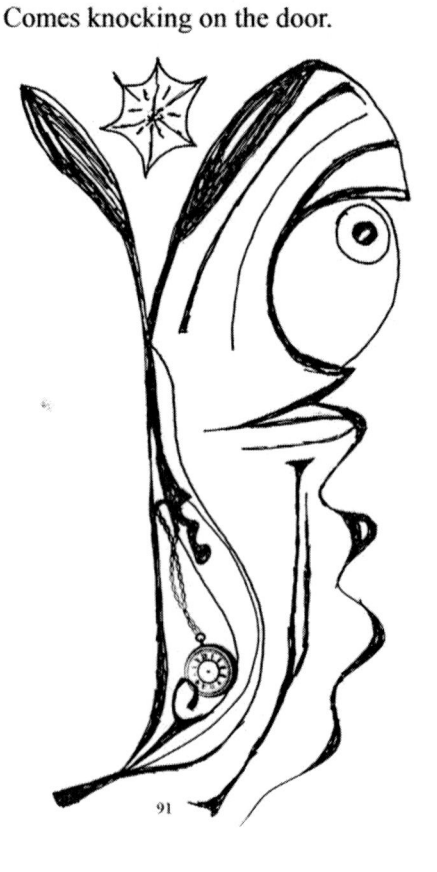

Comes knocking on the door.

Feeling up for it

When you feel up for it too

Unlike you it was up to you

When some other called you to bed

Bless ya! Bless ya! Is she tells me

All the same she does not call.

The point is dug in and hurting

The wounds will not stop oozing

Let us lie now to reality

So the monsignor said.

Come in to her room

To her that must be obeyed .

It all broke in on her mind one day

Where in the world she lived

She left

A bed of despair.

Father closed the door gently

In his most well known loving way.

Gently with exhausted love.

Too soon she suspects a goodbye

Awesome your high stubborn birth.

You I know and that to look at you is beyond me now.

I am tired of insomnia so don't sedate me

I'm lazy enough

Put this first, put me first

Put the wish of me

Put us first now and always.

Truly through my eyes

There is no stress when wearing a dress

Strap on up your arse.

The conversations dried up

Since turning off the phone.

The silence is a horror

The ring tones aren't ringing

It's time to go to bed already.

She spoke these words. I'm dying
I'm dying.

I'm dying to retort

Yes now hush little baby don't you cry.

I told you at last

I feel great now I've told you

I love you and I told you I do too.

Now I think you wait
And that's not for me.

Give it some status for the strategy alone

To wish you goodbye

As you switch out the lights.

She properly thinks now

Go home loser and write a poem about it.

Its not possible to watch your eyes move

In the mirror.

The burning of a midnight lamp

Lights up the tick

On the watch face.

The watchman sees and listens too.

He will groan and go on

About his business.

He handles the lamp with ease

Cradled in his calloused hand.

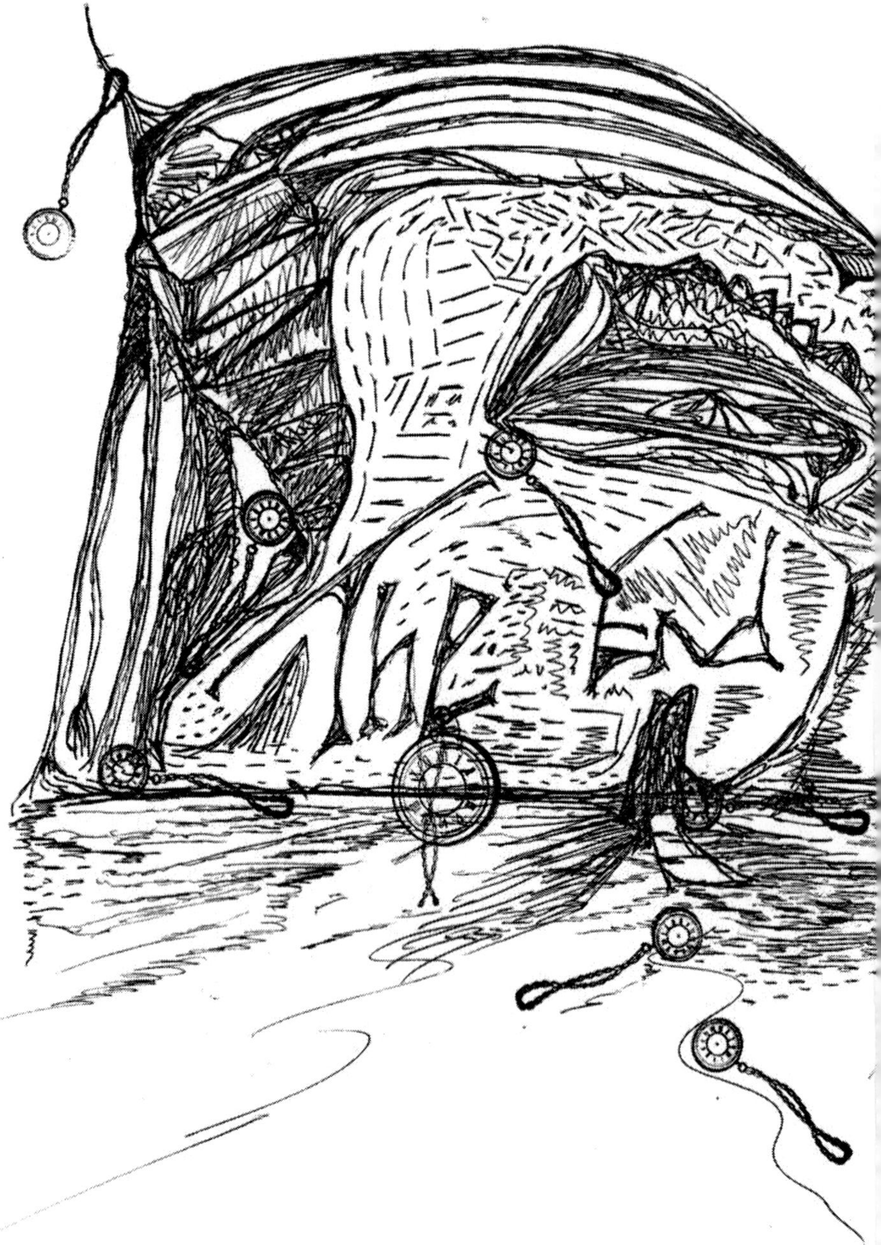